Lost in the Woods

Building a Life Up North

Richard Hill

Lost in the Woods

Building a Life Up North

By Richard Hill

Published by:
Gale Force Press
Sault Ste. Marie, Michigan

Editor: Tyler Tichelaar
Cover and Interior Design: Stacey Willey, Globe Printing

ISBN: 978-0-981-7371-4-0
Library of Congress: 2016906898

First Printing 2017

Every attempt has been made to source properly all quotes.
Disclaimer: While this book is based on true events, certain names have been changed to protect individuals' privacy.

Website: GaleForcePress.com

To all the independent souls in the world who like to experience things firsthand.

"Not till we are lost, in other words, not till we have lost the world, do we begin to find ourselves...."

— ***Thoreau,*** *Walden*

Books by Richard Hill

Lake Effect: A Deckhand's Journey on the Great Lakes Freighters

Hitchhiking After Dark: Offbeat Stories from a Small Town

Lost in the Woods: Building a Life Up North

Contents

Introduction 1

Chapter 1 - A Shot in the Dark 7

Chapter 2 - Germination 17

Chapter 3 - Taking Root 31

Chapter 4- Clearing the Land 45

Chapter 5 - Shelter 69

Color Photos 83

Chapter 6 - Branching Out 111

Chapter 7 - Old Neighborhoods 127

Chapter 8 - Briars and Brambles 137

Chapter 9 - Dry Rot 147

Chapter 10 - Hair of the Dog 163

Chapter 11 - What Goes Around 179

Notes 193

Timeline 197

Acknowledgments 198

Log Building Resources 199

About the Author 209

Introduction

Have you ever been driven to distraction by an obsession, a maddening compulsion that won't leave you alone? It could be a lingering idea that once crossed your mind, a loose thread of a long-forgotten conversation, or some vague sort of dream of pursuing a particular goal. Such was the case when my wife and I decided to leave the retail business world for a few years and embark on a journey of building a log home in Michigan's Upper Peninsula. Having talked about it off and on for several years, we were ready to move forward and put our plan into action. We would start life anew, work with our hands on a challenging enterprise, pursue a fresh business idea, and raise our growing family in the area where we had grown up. Our excitement soon grew to a fever pitch. The north woods was calling, and we couldn't wait to get started. It would be a monumental undertaking, a severe test of strength and will—none of which we truly understood at the time.

Moving up north, from Traverse City, my wife and I felt the need to escape from the hectic pace of running a retail shop in a busy shopping mall. Despite our growing success, the long hours and the sterile mall environment made us long for a new life. We wanted more authenticity in our lives, greater control over our working hours, and more involvement with our friends and local community. We longed to escape from the superficial mall atmosphere and make closer contact with nature. Although we were fortunate to be financially successful in business, we also sensed a nagging hollowness that something more important was missing, some essential piece of the puzzle that, if ignored, might elude us forever. Perhaps, if we couldn't climb to the top of Maslow's ladder, we could at least move up a couple of rungs and find more meaningful, self-actualized lives.

To this end, what captured our imagination most intensely was the ambition of moving to the Upper Peninsula (the U.P.) and building a log home along the shores of Lake Superior. This owner-built home, as we would learn, was a true hands-on experience of epic proportions, especially for a couple of eager neophytes. Every day of construction required countless decisions to be made. Not everything went exactly according to our "foolproof" blueprint. Quite often, we would have to improvise and make the necessary adjustments. I don't remember inviting Murphy and his troublesome in-laws to this project, but they came anyway and made themselves quite comfortable. We did our best to work around them.

Working with a variety of subcontractors was an education in itself. A written contract with all the details clearly spelled out is a wonderful thing to behold. It helps avoid specific arguments over details and prices that have already been agreed upon. However, in my naiveté, I trusted certain contractors to keep their word and was greatly disappointed when they didn't. Invoices were often inflated; people didn't show up for work when they were scheduled; sloppy work had to be redone. We might have steered clear of these problems had we put together a detailed and more clearly worded contract with each of the subcontractors. Handshake agreements, as I soon learned, don't carry much weight in the contracting world.

This entire log-building project was a venture into the unknown. There was so much more to understand than I had realized. Learning more about the intrinsic nature of building with logs—the inevitable movement, the unpredictable shrinking as they dried, the sheer mass of the material—became a valuable lesson in humility. Much of what I expected went right out the window. For instance, when it came to electrical wiring and plumbing runs, it was clear that this was not normal construction. Allowance would have to be made for the ways that logs move, twist, and shrink. Any experienced log home builder would ignore this caveat at his own peril.

With log construction, issues sometimes arise for which one has no clear frame of reference. Though it is usually more important to think things through, detail by detail, before acting, often there are times when one has to trust his gut instinct and go forward. It all comes down to one's ability to solve problems by being resourceful; the more experience one has, the more competent he or she becomes.

This experience of building a log home taught me how little I actually knew about the true meaning of persistence. Why, I wondered, does a person want to keep going forward in the face of mounting problems and frustrations? Why not throw in the towel and put it all behind you? My understanding seemed to evolve the more I contemplated the nature of work itself. By working with both my hands and my mind, I felt rewarded every time I was able to overcome an obstacle. The labors of log construction brought their own sense of spiritual fulfillment, not unlike the satisfaction I have felt making furniture.

In my late twenties, I was focused on the idea of making one-of-a-kind furniture for a living. For a while, I made small production runs of jewelry boxes, Swedish door harps, and Aztec drums over the winter months, then sold them at summer art fairs. Before long, I had earned a few commissions for smaller pieces of furniture, which afforded me the opportunity to expand my tool collection.

Living in a somewhat rural area in northern Lower Michigan, it didn't take me long to realize how difficult it was to eke out a living as a woodworker. The work itself was pure pleasure, but the reality was that my bills weren't getting any smaller. Working away contentedly in my shop, I loved the intoxicating aroma of cherry shavings as I planed the edge of a new piece of lumber and the delicate fragrance of ash when I ran it through my table saw. Like many fellow woodworkers, I soon discovered that I needed a day job to support my addictive habit.

When my wife and I took over a small retail kiosk in the local mall, we were able to market my remaining woodwork pieces on a daily basis. However, due to the rigors of managing a retail business full-time, virtually no idle hours remained for woodworking. I would have to put those skills on hold for the time being. The trade-off was that for the first time in our lives, we were now able to earn a decent living.

Fortunately for us, within seven years of working very diligently at our business, we were in a position to contemplate the building of a log home up north. It would be a return to woodworking, in a sense, but on a grander scale. In many ways, it was an attempt to find the good life, a search for more meaning in our everyday existence. Through manual labor, slowly constructing a dream piece-by-piece, we hoped to find more personal fulfillment by becoming completely immersed in the process. In the end, there were many more pluses than minuses. But along the way, the journey was full of pitfalls and surprises. It is my hope that telling this tale will shed light on what sort of experience the next person, if he shares a similar dream, might expect.

This is a story of trying to build a dream home on a tight budget by personally taking on most of the necessary work. It is not for someone with sufficient wealth to hire out the entire building process start to finish, although much can still be learned here. If there is steadfast persistence, good things usually come from the struggle. May our story bear humble witness.

[To track the order of events, please refer to the timeline at the back.]

Chapter 1

A Shot in the Dark

It ain't what you don't know that gets you into trouble.
It's what you know for sure that just ain't so.
— **Mark Twain**

A subzero winter's night. A handful of dying embers glow peacefully in the fieldstone fireplace, shooting a few stray sparks up the chimney. The warm living room air curls up the chimney into a white stream of smoke, rising through the snow-covered rooftop, then out into the starry night that watches over our newly built log home. My wife and I lie sound asleep in the upstairs bedroom, having put my two young boys to sleep hours ago.

Without warning, what sounds like a gunshot suddenly rings out in the night. From a dead sleep, my wife screams, then holds her breath, listening intently. I leap from the bed in the dark, startled, and bolt to the landing at the top of the stairs. *An intruder?* I wonder. *A prank of some kind?* I flip on the lights in the loft and rush to check on the boys. They haven't moved a muscle, seemingly lost in dreamful bliss. I quickly check the rooms downstairs and glance out the kitchen window to the lighted driveway, but nothing seems amiss.

For the life of me, I can't figure out where the sharp sound came from. I take a deep breath and slowly exhale. Since I'm awake anyway, I throw a few more chunks of birch and maple in the basement woodstove to stave off the ten-below-zero chill outside.

For three years now, we had been up to our eyeballs with the construction of this log house in Michigan's Upper Peninsula. And only a few months earlier, as winter was coming on, we had moved into this half-built log home. It is located on an acre lot covered mostly with spruce, white birch, and red maples on the eastern end of Lake Superior. Here, on the upper St. Mary's River, about a mile out in the channel, the Great Lakes ore freighters pass upbound and downbound on their way to various ports.

A short time later, talking to some others more knowledgeable about log homes, I learned what the "shot" was that I'd heard that night. What sounded like the sharp crack of a rifle was, in fact, the sudden release of pent-up tension in the logs as they lost their moisture over the winter from the heat of the wood furnace. As the log walls slowly dried out, their weight caused them suddenly to settle until they reached stasis. We were told to expect more "shots" in the future since it would take at least two heating seasons to stabilize the logs.

The red pine logs used to construct this house were full logs, with an average butt diameter of eighteen inches. Many of the logs measured fifty feet in length. The timber had been cut in Lower Michigan six months earlier and partially air dried. So a considerable amount of moisture was still in them.

Without totally realizing what we were getting involved in, my family was plunging into a very complex project that would not only turn our lives upside down but would take us, I reluctantly admit, more than twenty years to complete. It would become a wake-up call and a reality check like we had never experienced before. More than a few times, we would question the outright madness of a dream that had once seemed so simple and straightforward.

After a great deal of hair-pulling and budget-tweaking, I would become my own general contractor and sub out the plumbing, electrical, and any carpentry I didn't feel comfortable doing myself. My goal was to commit myself totally to this life-size project and complete it. My time table, if I worked diligently, would be about two, maybe two-and-a-half years. By that point, we could move in and plan the start of our new business, the Whitefish Bay Furniture Company.

In hindsight, my reality goggles were so fogged up that it would be a long, hard road before my vision made any sense. The simple stuff, I soon learned, was never simple, and the so-called easy stuff was anything but. Sometimes, we have to learn the hard way, a trial by fire, as they say. Over the next several years, we would often feel burned out and nearly defeated from the weight of our undertaking. The work would become an obsession with a life of its own. And yet, from these ashes would arise a fresh perspective on our self-imposed limits, human resilience, and a deeper understanding of life's possibilities.

Throughout the better part of the 1980s, my wife Judy and I had been living in Traverse City in Northern Michigan. We had been running a very small but profitable crystal kiosk at the Cherryland Mall, which was, at that time, one of the hottest retail locations in Michigan. Our shop, Forever Yours, measured only twelve by fourteen feet and was situated in the middle of a very busy mall, near the water fountain. We bustled with customers seven days a week, selling pewter wizards, dragons, fantasy figurines, prisms, and jewelry—all of which used Austrian Swarovski crystals in their design. In the sunlight, the beautiful crystals sparkled and split sunbeams into a magnificent spectrum of rainbow colors that danced off the walls and lit up a room.

The store, by mall requirements, was open for business from ten in the morning until nine at night, six days a week. Then on Sundays, from noon to five. Open year-round except on New Year's Day, Easter, Thanksgiving, and Christmas, we usually had great traffic and, over time, a very thriving business. My wife Judy, I soon discovered, was an unusually talented salesperson. Within a few years, we had become Cherryland Mall's most successful kiosk. Though the rent was quite steep every month, our brisk sales made it all worthwhile. On top of the base rent, we were required to pay a percentage rent when our sales rose above a certain level. So the Cherryland Mall made a generous profit off us as well.

In the late 1980s, the mall was a thriving, heavily trafficked venue. In the winter, customers came there to escape the frigid outside weather; in the summer, they flocked to the mall for air-conditioned heat relief. Business was brisk enough that we quickly managed to pay off our college loans and save enough for a small down payment to buy our first house.

We felt we were taking a substantial risk by signing a five-year land contract to purchase our first home. For one thing, our lease for the mall kiosk was for only six months at a time, even though we renewed it regularly. The mall, for whatever reason, refused to sign a longer one, which could have left our business in serious jeopardy if the management decided not to renew.

However, my wife and I had grown tired of living in small, cramped three-room apartments for the past seven years. By May of 1984, we had saved enough money for a modest down payment and purchased an aluminum-sided bi-level in a subdivision on the outskirts of Traverse City. Situated in the sandy remnants of an old cherry orchard, this house was a roomy vanilla box nestled among a surplus of young growing families. Although this starter home had the charm and personality of a loaf of white bread, it was, nevertheless, our first home; we were very excited to have a place of our own, a private yard, and a two-car garage.

With our short-term leasing arrangement at the mall, we felt no sense of job security, knowing the rug could be yanked from beneath us at any moment. The mall considered us a temporary kiosk, not a permanent inline store; so we were treated with second-class status. Consequently, we felt a bit nervous taking on the financial obligations of owning a house for the first time. As a result, we became quite self-sufficient and developed a tendency to save every dollar for the proverbial rainy day.

Eventually, it was time to upgrade a few things. One day we splurged on a "new" car, a five-year-old Honda Civic with a five-speed stick shift, a tiny toy of a car that drove like a Maserati. We had been making do with a fifteen-year-old Plymouth Valiant that was on its last legs. Everything about that car was threadbare and shaky: the vinyl upholstery was badly torn and blue smoke belched from the tailpipe. The Honda was the first truly reliable car we had ever owned. With so much uncertainty in our working lives, it was a relief to have something solid we could depend on for once.

Still, we continued to follow a thrifty lifestyle and felt the need to save up enough cash to act as a cushion should the mall refuse to renew our six-month lease. But seven years of success eventually took its toll. Any mom-and-pop business that operates seven days a week has virtually no opportunity for down time. As a hands-on business, my wife and I rarely had an opportunity to get away for more than a couple of days at a time. We had hired three part-time employees to help run the shop. As happy as we were with the business' success and all the wonderful people we had met, the relentless pace was sucking the life out of us. We felt chained to the Cherryland Mall. Something had to give.

By this time, we had a three-year-old boy and wanted to spend more time with him. If we started another business somewhere, we would establish our own schedule and not be bound by official mall hours. Something inside both of us seemed to call out for a new direction, a more humane pace of life, far away from the artificial fluorescent lights and the ever-present Muzak that droned endlessly from the mall's speakers. We liked the retail business, but not on the mall's terms.

Anything "up north" has always appealed strongly to anyone living in Lower Michigan. To those who live in the southernmost part of the state, "up north" means places like Traverse City to Gaylord, or areas close to the Mackinac Bridge. But to us, "up north" always meant the U.P., Michigan's Upper Peninsula. Those two words have usually signified relaxation, entertainment, and simply getting away from the world's many distractions and problems.

Since Judy and I were both natives of the Eastern U.P., many of our relatives still resided there. We had always loved the amenities and opportunities in the Traverse City area, while at the same time, so many intangibles were associated with living in the U.P. How would we make a living? Would the social isolation be tolerable? And though the relocation wasn't all that much further north, would the longer winters be bearable?

After lengthy consideration of all of our options, we finally decided to list the business for sale with a realtor. Although our retail business was just a small but simple kiosk in the middle of the mall, we had built up a great track record over the course of seven straight years. Many other seasonal kiosks came and went during the Christmas holiday season, but we remained there twelve months a year, mainly due to our steady sales volume. The mall had its own financial interest in our success. After paying a steep monthly base rate for rent, and the additional percentage rent on sales over a certain monthly volume, it's safe to say that the mall owners were happy with the numbers we were producing.

Through our realtor, we soon learned that none of the local banks would finance a loan for the sale of our business. According to the banks, they were reluctant to loan money to a "blue sky enterprise," any establishment that didn't own its own real estate. However, right next to our store in the mall, an inline chain store known as The Coffee Beanery had recently been listed for sale for $250,000 with only a two-year track record in Cherryland Mall. We, on the other hand, were a thriving business with a seven-year history. It made absolutely no sense. The only way to sell our shop was by financing the sale ourselves through a five-year land contract.

The advertisement was a so-called "quiet" listing in which only the local realtors knew the business was up for sale. Nothing appeared in the daily Multiple Listing Service (MLS). This setup would avoid many potential questions from curious customers as well as awkward explanations about why we were selling the shop.

The first summer we listed the business, we had several nibbles but no serious bites. But by the following spring (1990), we found a solid buyer who had recently retired from a downstate insurance business and was looking for a new venture. He and his wife purchased the business on a five-year land contract for what we felt was a reasonable price, but at the same time, more than we had ever dreamed of just a few years earlier. We had successfully mined that vein for seven years, and now we had the itch to stake a new claim somewhere else.

As soon as the closing papers were signed, we called Maple Island Log Homes, the company we had chosen to work with, and told it to go ahead with our construction plans. Everything seemed to be falling in place, and my wife and I were as happy as we had ever been. We had waited a long time to start building a new home, a new business, and a new life up north.

We were quite excited by the overall grandness of the plan. At last, we could take charge of our destiny and no longer be the pawns of outside forces. As we shifted gears, we began to realize that working for ourselves, come what may, seemed to fit our temperaments perfectly. In our own business, we would make all the choices and live with the consequences. It was a calculated risk we were willing to take. The uncertainty and mystery of what was to come next in our lives was both unnerving and mesmerizing.

Along with the initial down payment on the business, we would be receiving an ample monthly installment, then a lump sum at the end of the five-year land contract. I planned to complete the building of our log home within two years, doing much of the finishing work myself. At that point, our plan was to move in to the finished log home and start up our new retail store, a ready-to-finish furniture store to be named Whitefish Bay Furniture. I would custom-finish solid wood furniture and eventually design some of my own pieces for the store that local woodworkers could build in small production runs. This type of work would feel much more challenging and engaging than the many years spent working in a superficial mall setting. My degree was in art and design, with a concentration in furniture design. Now I could harness that background and put it to work for me.

My wife Judy would focus on the sales and display end of our new business. She had developed a great way with customers and seemed to thrive on all the social interaction of the sales floor. My responsibilities would mainly be centered on ordering new products, keeping the books, and custom-finishing the wood furniture. We would both share in the hiring and training of new employees as well as any other tasks that came along.

As anxious as we were to get the new enterprise off the ground, we realized that Whitefish Bay Furniture was at least two years away. Meanwhile, we had to finalize our log home construction plans and put them out for bids. Little did we know that the next several years would become one of the most exasperating and trying times of our lives. Just as things were starting to brighten up, our fortunes were about to take an unexpected turn.

Chapter 2

Germination

Don't judge each day by the harvest you reap, but by the seeds you plant.

— Robert Louis Stevenson

By July 1, 1990, we had turned over the keys to the new owners of our business. For the first time in seven years, we were free to move in a new direction, unburdened by any stray thoughts of employees, inventory, or sales goals. Our focus was now on finalizing the design for our log home in the north woods.

Once Maple Island Log Homes had been given the go-ahead, things quickly began to fall into place. When the blueprints were finally approved, the construction crews at the Muskegon log yard would start to pre-build the log walls in two sections: the first floor layout, then the second floor, including roof purlins and dormers. They would then number the logs, disassemble them, and truck them from the log yard to the Upper Peninsula sometime around mid-October. That is rather late in the season to be starting construction of this kind, especially with winter weather only a few weeks away. But we were too impatient to wait any longer and wanted to get this project underway so we could work on it over the winter months. Of course, in hindsight, waiting until spring would have been the prudent thing to do. Any kind of construction in snow country is always twice as difficult in wintertime.

We chose to work with Maple Island for several reasons. It offered a full-log style with an eighteen-inch average butt diameter red pine log. These were quite sizeable logs and would give the house a massive lodge-like appearance. The company claimed its logs were hand-peeled, but when they arrived on site, the logs appeared to have been mechanically debarked. The logs showed a regular pattern of chatter marks rather than a smooth hand-peeled profile. These would eventually have to be ground down with a power sander to make way for a smoother finish, a very time-consuming, labor-intensive project that we would underestimate.

We had been impressed with the company's model log home in Suttons Bay, a beautiful and charming log structure that was built with enormous twenty-two-inch diameter logs. Standing in the midst of this incredible structure, it seemed that the only thing missing was Paul Bunyan and Babe the Blue Ox. At this particular time, Maple Island did not offer a turnkey operation. In other words, once the log walls and roof framework were erected, we would have to take over from there and hire a general contractor to complete the structure.

Before settling on a final home design, Judy and I had done our due diligence. Our homework involved reading up on the many log options available from various log home companies. One choice, the double tongue-and-groove log, was flattened slightly on the top and bottom of the log and double-slotted for wood splines. In this way, the logs were both aligned and reinforced as the walls grew in height.

The D-log design involved flattening the log on three sides, leaving the roundness of one side for the building's exterior. Also, this design created a flat wall surface on the interior walls, a practical consideration when it came to hanging pictures or avoiding the potential for collecting dust.

There was also the Scandinavian-scribed-log style of building, known as Swedish-cope, in which each full-length successive log is hand-scribed to fit the profile of the log it is resting on. This very labor intensive process requires some first-rate woodworking skills.

The log style we eventually chose was the chinked log design. The red pine logs, over fifty feet in length and averaging eighteen inches in butt diameter, would be carefully fitted to be as level and close together as possible. For reinforcement, the log ends would be saddle-notched at the corners. To keep the walls somewhat level and balanced aesthetically as the building grew in height, the logs would alternate from one end to the other—first the butt end, then the narrower tapered end.

Once the walls were completely assembled, the chinking process would begin. Ethafoam, a material similar to Styrofoam but more flexible, would be stapled into place in the gaps between logs both inside and outside, leaving a dead-air space between the logs. The Ethafoam could be cut into various widths between one and three inches on the table saw, allowing a fifteen-degree bevel on the edge in order to fit the logs more closely. The long and tedious process of carefully spreading the chinking material would then follow.

Of course, some types of log home construction are much costlier than others. Initially, we had chosen the Scandinavian-scribe process, but we changed our minds when we were told that the chinked style would price out at about 20 percent less. Looking back now, that decision was a costly miscalculation. As we soon discovered, the cost of the chinking material and the many long hours spent applying it more than swallowed up any anticipated savings. It was another major hit to our ballooning budget.

Then again, we had to remind ourselves that if we were going to go to all the trouble to build this log house, we wanted it to be an authentic, handcrafted piece of work. At that time, we didn't realize that by choosing to build a chinked-style full-log house, we were committing ourselves to many long months of chinking that would stretch years into the future as various rooms in the house were finished. Aesthetically, chinked logs are very pleasing, but so much extra labor. We would eventually work our way through nearly fifty five-gallon buckets of Perma-Chink at the cost of over $100 per bucket. I might also mention the loss of a dozen pairs of blue jeans, sweatshirts, and T-shirts—all of which became trash once you got chinking on your clothes; they simply couldn't be laundered again. This gritty, putty-like material with latex added to it was worse than having chewing gum stuck to everything. Perma-Chink certainly lived up to its name.

In retrospect, in terms of time and money, the Scandinavian-scribe style would have been a much wiser choice. With this style, the only significant extra step would have been to apply a bead of caulking to the horizontal inside and outside joints where the logs met each other. By comparison, this step would have required only about 10 percent of the labor necessary for chinking.

One other log option we refused to consider was the half log. Basically, this method employed conventionally-framed two-by-four walls with half-log siding attached to the exterior. To us, it looked cheap and inauthentic, like some discounted, bargain-basement variety. If this was someone's idea of a log home, why even bother? Then there was the nine-inch, lathe-turned cedar logs, too thin to provide much R-value. They reminded us of Tinker Toys or Lincoln Logs, a toy house that hardly came close to our vision of a genuine year-round log home. The Three Little Pigs could have constructed a more attractive dwelling.

Overall, the closest competitor to the chinked style that we briefly considered was the full twelve-inch-diameter log made by Hiawatha Log Homes out of Munising, Michigan. These logs were turned on a giant lathe. Their product would have made an attractive and substantial log home, but, for our taste, everything about the design was too symmetrical and perfect. It had none of the charming irregularities and rough-hewn appearance of the chinked style we had finally chosen. Until we started researching log home designs and visiting various log home owners in our area, we had no idea such a wide variety of construction styles was available. We spent several years sorting it all out. It practically goes without saying that my wife and I were very cautious by nature and were obviously working within a tight budget. Living within our means was taking on a completely new context.

We drooled regularly over the gorgeous glossy log-home magazines that displayed beautiful color photos of sprawling log homes overlooking lush mountains and streams. These, we decided, were for wealthy business tycoons who could afford to throw several million dollars at whatever their hearts desired. But these log layouts were totally unrealistic and unattainable for the average family. Their only worth to us was for details and ideas, all of which would have to be scaled back drastically to be feasible.

Maple Island put us in touch with one of its log home designers. A soft-spoken, middle-aged fellow with many years of experience working as a home builder around Michigan, Bob lived in the Traverse City area. He had been commissioned by Maple Island to draw up blueprints for a variety of custom-designed log homes, all of which required a long list of special construction criteria.

Some of the essential things to be considered included: the bearing weight of solid log walls, the shrinkage of logs surrounding windows and doors, and the placement of interior partition walls. A log home is a completely different animal; it does not follow conventional rules. Settling of the walls over the next two heating seasons must be taken into account when laying out plumbing runs and electrical wiring. Space for settling above all windows and doors must be considered. Interior stud wall partitions have to "float" where they meet a log wall. And kitchen cabinets must be mounted independent of the log wall if they are to be stable.

We soon learned that log construction presents an entirely new set of problems that demands unique solutions. In fact, so many special details must be considered that many building contractors stay as far away as possible from log-home construction—too many unknowns and hair-pulling possibilities.

Over the course of the previous winter, I had met with Bob to work out an affordable home design. We were working with a budget that was clearly on the lean side. We wanted to design a log house that not only looked and felt authentic, but one that took into consideration our individual preferences and lifestyle. If Judy and I were willing to go to this much bother and expense, we wanted this place to exude high quality and integrity in every detail, and, of course, all on a budget.

The site we had selected, about a year earlier, for building this log home was about ten miles west of Sault Ste. Marie (commonly called "the Soo" by locals). It was situated at the foot of Isaac Walton Bay, sometimes known locally as Mosquito Bay, on the eastern end of Lake Superior. Only four or five houses were scattered throughout the immediate area, quiet and peaceful enough to offer privacy and remote enough for a rustic log home. We purchased a lot that measured 115 feet wide by 390 feet deep. Thickly wooded with spruce, white birch, and red maple, the property sloped abruptly 150 feet down to the lake, near the back of the lot. Over the coming years, this steep hillside feature would provide more than a vigorous workout for all of us as we struggled to haul armloads of firewood to the top, and to maneuver kayaks and canoes up and down this steep incline.

A mile or so across the bay was the sandy shore of Canada as well as a glowing red beacon, Point Louise, a navigational aid that helped guide the passing lake freighters safely through the shipping channel. It seemed like the perfect setting to start a log home dream—only ten miles from town, yet remote enough to offer both solitude and the proximity of a few neighbors. The final three miles leading to this property meandered down a gravel road that was good driving in the winter but a swirling dust bowl by midsummer whenever another vehicle passed.

When I made my weekly visit to Bob's house in TC (Traverse City) to discuss building plans, the first thing he would do was put a pot of coffee on the stove using his old-fashioned percolator. He would pop a couple of strong Arabica beans in his mouth and slowly chew them. Then he would toss in a couple of French Roast beans to tweak the mix. He crunched the robust combination thoughtfully, insisting on finding just the right blend when he made his coffee. This was always the first order of business each afternoon before settling down to work.

Once the coffee was perked and we had each poured a cup, we sat around the dining room table with the blueprints spread out. We began by roughing out some ideas for the most important features and details that we wanted to include in the design. For starters, we had wanted three bedrooms—the larger master bedroom with its own bathroom, a second bedroom for the kids, and a third bedroom to use as a music room. My wife Judy played guitar, I played drums, and we were planning on picking up a console piano sometime soon.

The dining room and kitchen should be reasonable size and perhaps designed as one room, divided by a raised counter with stools for seating. It would be convenient for the cook to be able to stay in conversational touch with his or her company during meal preparations. So an open concept would provide a better opportunity for social interaction.

The living room needed to be a decent size to accommodate small gatherings and perhaps an occasional jam session with our musician friends. For a bold statement, the living room also needed a cathedral ceiling and a fieldstone fireplace. We wanted sunlight coming through the kitchen windows every morning and lots of light generally in all the rooms. That detail would require the placement of skylight roof windows in several key spots. We would like to have hardwood floors in the living room, ceramic tile in the hallways, bathrooms, and kitchen/dining area. The only carpeting would be in the three bedrooms, partly because we were reluctant to vacuum. The house would be primarily heated with a wood furnace in the basement and, as a backup, electric baseboard heat in every room, each controlled by its own thermostat.

Plenty of other details needed to be worked out, but this preliminary list would get the ball rolling. Within a few weeks, Bob had completed the initial sketches of possible room layouts and exterior profiles. When I finally saw the first set of actual blueprints with various elevations, drawings of the log house's exterior from all four sides, I was absolutely thrilled. The whole process was suddenly a reality and not some distant dream.

As time went on, we talked about a few ballpark building estimates, and the dream quickly began to vaporize. Bob felt that this 2500-square-foot plan, at over $100 per square foot, might easily come in upwards of $300,000! That number was way beyond our working budget. We had hoped to finance this project incrementally through the monthly payments we received from our business' sale. In order to avoid any bank loans, we would have to rein in some major expenses. So it was back to the drawing board to see what could be cut.

To save money, many of the original details would have to be altered. One idea was to construct the entire first floor using full logs, then switch to conventional framing with two-by-four construction on the second floor. We could then go with some kind of wood siding to keep everything looking rustic on the exterior. Another idea was to reduce the square footage of the living room and bedrooms slightly. Here we encountered one of the main design difficulties of working with full logs. In our layout, the solid wall that divided the dining room/kitchen area from the living room stretched from the ground floor to the roof over the second floor, a height of nearly twenty-two feet. However, the master bedroom was situated directly above the dining room. So there was no way of reducing the size of that bedroom without also reducing the size of the dining/kitchen area directly beneath it. In conventional framing with lumber, you can place a partition wall wherever you like. But in this particular instance, the log wall had to move as one unit.

Another major concern with log home building is hiding the plumbing pipes between the first and second floors. They have to line up with each other vertically. So partition walls have to line up accordingly, first floor with second floor. Plumbing pipes cannot be hidden within the solid outside log walls of the building. Also, settling of the log walls must be taken into account when the plumbing runs are designed. Now I realize why most plumbers shy away from log home construction: too much frustration, way too many variables.

Electrical contractors don't have it much easier either. They have to drill vertical runs through solid logs and sneak horizontal runs behind the chinking material. Electrical outlet boxes and switch boxes have to be drilled out and hand-chiseled in all log walls, a very time-consuming process. It often takes a creative electrician with some handy woodworking skills to solve some of the challenges that present themselves.

All winter long, Judy and I worked to reduce the square footage from 2500 to just over 2000. But in the end, we were not happy with any of the new layouts. The rooms were much smaller; the kitchen was moved to the north side of the house, where there would be no sunlight, rather than the previous location on the southeast corner. The flow of the rooms was simply a poor substitute for the original layout.

Finally, we decided to return to our original plans and try to find other hands-on ways to cut costs. Bob advised us to give the blueprints to five different building contractors for estimates. He encouraged us to throw out the highest bid, mainly because it was too costly and would probably lack a lot of specific detail. Sometimes, he cautioned us, the high bidder was just trying to make a killing and hadn't spent a great deal of time crunching the numbers. Bob also recommended throwing out the lowest bidder because that guy most likely missed a whole slew of details that would eventually have to be paid for. The three bids in the middle were the ones to take seriously.

Over the next several months, I contacted builders in the Soo area. One builder tried to talk me completely out of the use of logs for a home. He said, "There's a hell of a lot of lumber you could get for $40,000," the cost of the logs from Maple Island. To try to reduce our costs, we compared the high price of using all Marvin brand windows with true divided lights to a similar but less expensive package from Weather Shield: a significant savings.

Another very reputable builder in the area came in about $75,000 over our budget. I'm sure he would have done a first class job on the project, but we couldn't afford him. We asked a third builder to price everything out except the finishing on the interior and exterior. We thought perhaps we could do the staining, varnishing, and painting ourselves to save a few dollars. Still, the bid came in too high.

By this time, we had worked our way through three different sets of blueprints, trying to whittle down the estimated bids. The construction companies bidding were all outfits with reasonable log home building experience. From talking to a number of families who lived in log homes, we had learned how foolhardy and costly it would be if we hired a construction company with absolutely no log-building experience. The workers would be learning all the complexities of log construction while they were on the job, but at our expense. As much as possible, we wanted to avoid any shoddy work or poor craftsmanship.

After a great deal of soul-searching and hair-pulling, we felt the need to return to the original design. There was no point in dreaming of a magnificent log house if the final result was some bland rendition of our original plan. The more I thought about what I would be paying a general contractor to do, the more I began to wonder whether we could pull this whole thing off by ourselves. By hiring a builder, I would be paying for his experience and skill not only to complete the final construction, but to subcontract the other necessary skilled workers: the excavator, the electrician, the plumber, the carpenter, roofers, masons, furnace installers, and so forth. After much careful thought, I decided at last to become my own general contractor. We would work slowly and methodically, step by step, and try to make this project fit our budget.

My background was in furniture design, so I had a fair amount of experience with carpentry and woodworking tools. I could also handle some simple plumbing tasks and basic electrical work. To fill in the holes, I planned to purchase a few trade manuals on drywall, roofing, and tiling as I needed them. By subcontracting the jobs that I couldn't handle, I would conceivably be able to save a bundle of money.

The individual bids by subcontractors would have to be proposed again, this time on a specific job-by-job basis. Everything would have to be broken down into smaller, more manageable parts. And most importantly, contracts would need to be worked out and signed. As Tracy Kidder so wisely pointed out in *House*, his study on home building:

> The written agreement separates emotions from transactions. If you put your deal in writing, you can head off misunderstanding and deter malfeasance. . . . In every era, significant numbers of people have prepared for the construction of houses as they have prepared for death, by getting their wishes down in writing.[1]

In hindsight, I learned that contracts need to be very detail specific with regard to work expectations. And yet misunderstandings still arise. Whenever money is involved, it's always prudent to get it down on paper—some good advice that, sadly, I did not adhere to 100 percent and lived to regret.

Without a doubt, this owner-built plan would require a much longer time frame. A typical construction loan from a bank might allow up to six months for complete building construction. However, since we were receiving monthly payments from the sale of our business, my wife and I could take our time and work on this log home project at our own pace. The business payments were scheduled to last for five years, and we had hoped to finish the house within two to three years and then start up the new Whitefish Bay Furniture Company. We weren't sure whether we could handle the technical complexities and stresses of completing a log home by ourselves, but we decided to go for it. It was the only possible way we would be able to afford it. We had no idea yet of the total craziness we were about to get into during the next few years. But we felt a great sense of confidence and passion in our ability to resolve problems as they appeared. Myriad snags and obstacles would need to be overcome soon enough, joys of accomplishment as well as frustration from the unforeseen and unexpected. A good sense of humor and humility would become invaluable, but stubbornness and persistence would prove to be our saving grace.

Chapter 3

Taking Root

A man is but the product of his thoughts. What he thinks, he becomes.
— **Mohandas K. Gandhi**

Ever since our college days, the idea of someday, when our budget allowed, building an alternative shelter had always intrigued Judy and me. We thought about buying a piece of land with a south-facing hill to build an earth shelter, a living space carved into the side of a large grassy slope. There seemed to be so many advantages to this kind of structure. No matter what climate, the earth maintained a steady temperature of around fifty degrees. So the cost of heating would be minimal. The solar gain from facing a southerly direction would also help to cut costs. Besides, saving on fossil fuels was also very Earth-friendly. But the more I thought about this idea, the more I felt like a hobbit living underground, not to mention the creepy feeling of claustrophobia or possibly being trapped underground in some catastrophic cave-in.

Next, we looked into the possibility of constructing an octagonal house or something along the lines of a geodesic dome, an idea no doubt inspired by the intriguing designs of Buckminster Fuller. A house built octagonally, while using the same amount of lumber for the perimeter of the construction as a smaller rectilinear plan, can increase the square footage significantly, by as much as 20 percent. Many of the geodesic designs we looked at used an open floor plan in which one living space flowed naturally into the next, with the need for very few partition walls. The drawback to this layout was that sound, as well as dust, also flowed naturally from room to room. There was no place to go for any sense of privacy or solitude. Domes, we decided, are great for their simplicity, but they have limited practical function.

While we were living in Traverse City, we became intrigued by the idea of renovating an old church or schoolhouse. Perhaps somewhere in the past, this idea germinated from watching Arlo Guthrie in that old hipster movie *Alice's Restaurant*; I can't be sure. With luck, we were able to track down two old schoolhouses in our vicinity. The first was halfway up the Old Mission Peninsula and seemed to be in reasonable shape. It was sided in paint-blistered white clapboard and proudly boasted two walls of tall windows overlooking a farmer's field. The belfry was still intact, though it appeared to be sharing space with a family of pigeons. The building had been sadly neglected for forty-some years. The second schoolhouse was situated near the corner of what is now the Grand Traverse Mall. The building was small and simple and could be purchased for a mere $3000.

Of course, in hindsight, we should have bought at least one of these properties. But, in the real world, we had neither the money nor the time for major renovations, though that didn't stop us from dreaming. Our business was too time-consuming even to think about taking on a new project. I believe the schoolhouse up on the peninsula eventually became a beautifully-restored wine-tasting shop for one of the local vineyards.

Another prospect we considered was to purchase a train car

and convert it into a living quarters. People have been turning railroad cars into diners and museums for many years, so this seemed like a very cool and eccentric way to live. The practical side of this dream was that conversion—with all the heating, plumbing, and electrical work—would cost considerably more than we ever anticipated, not to mention the great expense of moving an enormous train car to our location.

The entire reason for mentioning all of these offbeat choices for a future home is to show clearly that, for a long time, we were interested in designing an unconventional structure, something that had a dream quality about it, something very distinctive and personal. All of us dream about the things we really want, even if they are impractical or remote. It's a vital part of who we are—anticipating, hoping for something elusive and magical in the future. As Michael Pollan points out in *A Place of My Own*:

> Daydreaming does not enjoy tremendous prestige in our culture, which tends to regard it as unproductive thought . . . . The very process of daydreaming is pleasurable. And, I would guess, is probably a psychological necessity . . . . Daydreaming is where we go to cultivate the self . . . out of view and earshot of other people.[2]

In music and art, daydreaming is the state in which some of the most vibrant work is created. So, in a sense, designing a living space that we would feel comfortable in was at least as psychological as it was physical.

A house begins as a vision, an attempt to make tangible many of our wants and desires. Gaston Bachelard, in his book *The Poetics of Space*, must have felt the same way: "The house shelters daydreaming, the house protects the dreamer, the house allows one to dream in peace."[3] Our house would become our sanctuary, a place we would retreat to for safety, comfort, and a sense of solitude.

As younger kids, my friends and I spent many summers building neighborhood forts, tree houses, and clubhouses out of miscellaneous boards and odd pieces of lumber found in alleyways. We built forts with trap doors on six-foot-high stilts, to keep out any undesirables. One morning, my friends and I arrived at our tree fort and found an official citation tacked to the door. Apparently, the city building inspector was none too impressed by our newly developed carpentry skills. The notice complained that our fort was in strict violation of the city building code and the property owner was threatened with a severe fine if the structure were not removed promptly. Some people, we thought, take their jobs way too seriously. So we ignored the citation and went about our boyhood business.

At times, we hammered together a tree fort with actual "wall-to-wall" carpeting, which we nailed to ceiling, walls, and floors alike. Somehow, we had overlooked the simple necessity of waterproofing the roof, only to find, after a driving rainstorm, that moldy carpeting did not make a very hospitable clubhouse. But, as kids, we desired a place of our own for secret meetings and conversations about taboo subjects, far away from the prying eyes and ears of nosy parents.

Looking back now, I wonder why Judy and I didn't simply move to the Soo and purchase a decent existing house in a good neighborhood—something we could refurbish and put our individual stamp on. There were several attractive historic homes around town at reasonable prices, some of

Victorian design as well as a few salt-box variations. Even a few charming waterfront homes were available on the Lower St. Mary's River. Surely, choosing that route would have been so much easier and less costly than starting a building project from scratch. But love is blind, and building a log home is no exception.

In Traverse City, we had taken an enormous step moving from a cramped apartment to a relatively roomy house. We had repainted most of the rooms and planted a small garden out back. This particular bi-level, however, had very few outstanding amenities, but it was a welcome change from the renting treadmill. After living there for a few years, we began to dream of someday having a house with a fireplace, a separate dining room, larger bedrooms, and if we were lucky, a breathtaking view of the countryside. One could only do so much with an aluminum-sided square box lined with drywall and shag carpeting. Best of all, however, our $425 monthly payment was very affordable.

About this time, worrying that we might someday abruptly lose our business at the mall for lack of a long-term lease, we began to search for alternative options for employment. It just so happened that Traverse City was home to the Great Lakes Maritime Academy where officers were trained for engine room and deck jobs on the lake freighters. Until then, that had not meant much to me. In previous years, I had sailed as a deck hand and deck watch on several ore carriers and had enjoyed the work and lifestyle, even if it were a bit lonely at times. We had routinely carried cargoes of iron ore and limestone from ports like Duluth and Cedarville to lower Great Lakes destinations such as Chicago, Cleveland, and Conneaut. As the summer went by, I began to daydream of a possible career as a mate (deck officer) aboard the freighters. I would make a good salary, have winters off, and be able to spend time out on the Great Lakes in all seasons—a memorable experience I had always relished. I soon found myself checking out the required courses and costs involved in attending Northwestern Michigan College (NMC), home of the maritime academy. Within six months, by June of 1985, I was back in school.

I hadn't realized how much I missed the stimulation of an academic environment until I returned. I was hungry to learn again and eagerly lapped up the classroom experience and textbooks like a thirsty seadog. Along with a large number of cadets, fresh from high schools across the country, I was one of the few "senior" students in attendance, now in my early thirties, but I didn't mind a bit.

The following summer, I climbed aboard the *Columbia Star* as a second-year cadet. I had always wanted to work aboard a thousand-footer on the Great Lakes, and this was to be my first and only chance. I roomed with a third-year engine cadet who already had his Third Mate's license. Our living quarters were situated on the ship's stern, with all the other after-cabins, one deck below the pilothouse.

The overall size of the ship was quite impressive, more than three football fields in length. On peaceful evenings out on the lakes, we found ways to entertain ourselves—some crewmembers rode their bicycles in laps around the enormous deck; others played Trivial Pursuit or poker in the galley. A few of the engineers, on warm Sunday afternoons, brought out golf clubs and balls and drove them into the wild blue yonder. Surrounded by water, cooped up inside the ship most of the day, we found it a great relief to take a summer stroll in the "park" whenever possible.

As usual, the quality of the food aboard ship was incredible—from lake trout and T-bone steaks to stuffed pork chops and hot-buttered corn on the cob. Every morning, the second cook delighted the crew by baking fresh chocolate chip cookies, savory hot-cross buns, and mouth-watering blueberry muffins. With a menu like that, staying on a diet was hardly an option.

As a deck cadet, my captain's orders were to be present in the pilothouse whenever we entered port, approached the St. Mary's River or Detroit River systems, or locked through the Soo Locks. Otherwise, my time could be spent completing my written sea project, a set of assignments sent weekly from the academy.

On most afternoons, out in the middle of Lakes Superior and Michigan, I sat at a small steel desk in my cabin working to complete my sea project. As you might expect, the Spartan furnishings in my cabin were minimal: two steel bunks, welded to a steel deck, two metal chests of drawers bolted to the steel bulkhead, two metal lockers, and a vinyl-covered tubular-steel chair for comfort. A four-by-six-foot brown carpet remnant covered the steel deck between our bunks. After a while, you simply accepted living in this "iron house," where one had no say in the choice of accommodations. Although the room furnishings were austere, complemented by the stark fluorescent lighting overhead, we couldn't complain—the rent was free. It was one more place in the long list of offbeat housing I had lived in—the many substandard rentals in which I had grown up, the economy dorm room on campus, or the series of cramped three-room apartments we had coped with since marriage. Would I ever live, I wondered, in a place that was roomy, clean, and comfortable?

Within a month aboard the *Columbia Star*, I realized I was having a serious change of heart. The majesty and raw beauty of the Great Lakes still held an alluring attraction for me, but the job itself and some of the ship personnel made me see things from a new perspective.

Technology had modernized and improved the entire

prospect of ship navigation. The advent of Loran-C systems and other computer advancements had brought about great strides in Great Lakes shipping in the short twelve-year span since I had been a deckhand. So many of the previous skills necessary for a good mate to navigate across the lakes were now automated. Except for sharp navigational expertise in the rivers and coming into port, a mate's position was virtually reduced to that of a caretaker. He or she watched the many gauges, monitored the weather and the course, and kept a sharp eye on the radar and any other shipping traffic. At both ends of the lake, the mates were responsible for carefully loading and unloading the ship's cargo. However, there were often many long hours spent in the pilothouse as the ship slowly crossed an open lake. A more necessary survival skill, only too frequently, was being able to carry on a good conversation with the watchman and the wheelsman over the course of a four-hour watch.

One wheelsman I sailed with didn't care to talk much with the others but loved to whistle. The problem was he insisted on whistling the same tune, over and over again, for hours on end. Up in the pilothouse, whenever there was a lull in the mate's conversation, the wheelsman sensed his cue and launched into his favorite melody, whistling away until the mate finally exploded, "Stop! Don't you know any other goddamned tune but that? You're driving me nuts!" For a few days, the wheelsman would then lay low on his watch, but before long, he would revert to the mean and again began whistling his old familiar tune. Knowing there were only two more months until his vacation, the mate essentially gave up and took a vow of silence.

Over the course of several months, other troubling issues surfaced in the pilothouse, the ship's "brain box." At first, I hadn't realized what serious ego problems some of the mates on this ship had. Perhaps it was because the *Columbia Star* happened to be the flagship of the Columbia fleet, and all the top guns wanted a position aboard her. Some of the mates held captain's licenses and made sure all crewmembers were aware of it. Nevertheless, one could certainly sense the rivalry to show off in front of the old man. A lowly cadet could hardly make the slightest error without getting reamed by one of the mates.

Some days, as I stood near the pilothouse front window, I watched the three deckhands down on the spar deck making the ship ready for port. They methodically removed the hatch covers, made the boarding ladder ready, and prepared to swing over the ship's side, hanging on to the bosun's chair. Their hands-on job appealed to me more instinctively than I had ever expected. I couldn't help but compare the tension and boredom of the pilothouse to the carefree life of a deckhand. My days of apathy and disillusionment began to grow, and it was only a matter of time before I jumped this ship for good. This "iron house" was no longer home to me.

In August, 1986, I returned home to Traverse City from the lakes. My wife Judy, in her ninth month of pregnancy for our first child, and my cocker spaniel Raleigh, were so happy to see me. I resumed work at our Forever Yours kiosk in the mall and did what I could to help prepare for the imminent birth of our son. Months earlier, in the spring, we had attended Lamaze classes to learn the proper breathing and coaching techniques. The big moment was fast approaching.

When my wife's water broke at four o'clock on the morning of September 15, we flew out of bed in a frenzy, set the packed suitcase by the door, and began timing her contractions. By 6:00 a.m., it was getting light outside as a heavy drizzle began to fall. I glanced out into the driveway at my little red Honda Civic and remembered that I needed to repair the muffler that was dragging on the ground due to a broken clamp. As soon as a contraction ended, I raced out to the garage, raised the door, and drove the soggy vehicle inside for repair. Then I hurried back to the house just as another series of contractions was beginning. Holding my wife's hand, I tried to soothe her through the mounting pain, and then quickly sprinted back out to the garage. Beneath the Honda, with water dripping in my face from the dangling exhaust pipe, I wired the muffler to the frame with a coat hanger, looked at my watch, and raced back into the living room for another round.

By 9:00 a.m., I was dialing Dr. VanDalson at Munson Hospital, insisting that the baby was ready to pop, and that all hell was ready to break loose. He calmly reassured me that we had plenty of time and not to show up at the hospital until about two or three that afternoon. How he could be so cool and relaxed at a moment like this, I had no idea. The next few hours seemed like an eternity. For some odd reason, I did not want to be the first one on my block to deliver his own baby.

At 4:00 a.m., after twenty-four hours of labor, my son Travis was born. My wife was exhausted, and I was ready to keel over. But at that very moment, we felt a profound sense of exhilaration and peace like none other. It had all been worth it. I was relieved and thankful to be there in that hospital delivery room, at that crucial moment, rather than miles away on some Great Lakes freighter.

Out on the lakes, I had known many fathers who held respectable jobs aboard ship and yet were absent from their growing families for many long months of the year. While I was growing up, my father had been stationed in the U.S. Army at various bases around the country and, as a result, missed most of my childhood. I did not want to make that same mistake.

The birth of Travis added a sharp focus to our lives that had been missing. Like any new parents, we learned to juggle our schedule creatively to make room for our newest addition. Our newborn was a tangible reminder of what we had been working toward every day. We were amazed by how abruptly such a little person could transform our lives. More than anything, the birth of our first child focused our attention on providing a stable and substantial home environment in which he could grow up—unlike the shifting sands of so many low-life rentals in which I had lived as a child. With family in mind, our ideas and dreams of building seemed to be slowly taking root.

After living in TC for ten years, our family was ready to return to the Upper Peninsula, to rediscover our roots, to start over, in a sense. Having been married for thirteen years, we were tired of renting apartments and living in a nondescript bi-level. We had grown anxious to own a piece of Lake Superior waterfront where we could put our own individual stamp on something.

Having both been born in Sault Ste. Marie, Judy and I felt like salmon returning upstream. The move north was a conscious choice that we had considered long and carefully. We would be leaving behind a great number of friends, amenities, and opportunities in Traverse City. How, some of our friends wondered, could we even consider moving to such a desolate backwoods as the U.P.? What would we do for jobs? We calmly assured them that the Upper Peninsula, believe it or not, had readily-available running water, electricity, and the occasional delivery of a daily newspaper. We could somehow manage. The Soo was still only a three-hour drive away, but once you drive northward and cross the mighty Mackinac

Bridge, it's as if you've entered a pristine wilderness and left another world behind.

One reason for moving back was the immediate sense of family. Our kids would grow up knowing many of their aunts, uncles, and grandparents who lived in the nearby area. We hoped this regular family contact would give them a better sense of their roots and heritage. I grew up seeing my relatives only once every several years, and some I never met. My wife, on the other hand, coming from a large Italian family, was fortunate always to have many of her aunts, uncles, nieces, and nephews around. To this day, I still marvel at how well she can remember all of their names; for the life of me, I cannot keep them straight in my head.

Shortly after our first son Travis was born, I became keenly aware of establishing our own family traditions—the Christmas tree, Easter baskets, Halloween pumpkins, and so forth. Perhaps our new log home would someday become a gathering place for friends and family, not only for Thanksgiving celebrations, but for special occasions year-round. One family tradition I had always admired at my wife's parents' house when we were first dating was the weekly Sunday afternoon spaghetti dinner. On that very special day, the entire family gathered together for a feast of ravioli, cannelloni, or simply spaghetti and meatballs that was lovingly prepared for family, a few friends, and sometimes a stray uncle or aunt. The rich red tomato sauce was simmered all night long until it developed a thick tangy texture. The meal was an all-afternoon affair that included not just pasta, but salad, Italian bread, Paisano wine, and dessert. Sometimes, the family would take a break for an hour or so in the living room, to talk and tell a few stories, and then go back for round two. The food was always outstanding, and I grew to enjoy the leisurely ritual of taking an entire Sunday afternoon to savor the meal and one another's company. Nobody seemed to be in a hurry to go anywhere else; the food and conversation were that good. This was the kind of simple family tradition that bonded us all together, family and friends, and I only hoped we could one day establish our own special family rituals.

When all was finally said and done, why did we finally settle on a log home structure rather than a conventionally designed, or stick-built, home? It all traces back to the impressions of childhood that seem to stay with us for such a good long time and subtly influence so many of our choices. What we were after, it seems, was a design that had a handcrafted look about it, both inside and out, as well as a structure that brought out some of the magic of childhood.

Something about the primitive use of logs recalled for me my Finnish ancestors who were early residents of Upper Michigan. It was direct and simple. In a log house, one can see the construction details all about him; very little is concealed in the walls. It has a muscular quality about its design that imbues it with visual strength. Just as a kid takes pride in his handmade, improvised fort, humble as it is, we would hope someday to take pride in the handcrafted quality of each and every log detail. In an age of mass-produced sameness, it would be stimulating and fun to live in a space that was truly one of a kind.

We did not want to abandon our original plans strictly because of the unaffordable cost. By this time, we were consumed not just by the amount of effort we had expended but also by the considerable emotional investment we had made. It felt a little reckless to go forward with such a mammoth project, considering the potential financial mess we were flirting with. As Sarah Susanka puts it, in her study on building and design ideas, *The Not So Big House*: "Building a house, more than any other undertaking, pits our dreams against our realities. When we think about dollars we tend to be very practical. Dreams, by their very nature, are often impractical. The reconciliation of the two is never an easy thing."[4] Guided mainly by adrenaline and instinct, we were ready to take on Goliath with a sling shot and an anxious sense of adventure.

Chapter 4

Clearing the Land

An idea that is developed and put into action is more important than an idea that exists only as an idea.

— **Buddha**

A heavily wooded lot, strewn with overgrown spruce and jack pines, awaited us that summer. It was shortly after the Fourth of July when we arrived on site with our chainsaw and axes to begin clearing the building site. I had purchased a sturdy Homelite chainsaw that had enough muscle not to bog down from the many long hours of cutting and trimming now upon us. My brother Fred offered to help Judy and me with work on the chain sawing and site preparation. By late July, we were joined by Brennan, my fifteen-year-old nephew from Grand Rapids, up in the Soo for a few weeks to help us out.

The site was so overgrown with small balsams and birches that there was barely room to drop a tree cleanly to the ground. So we began by cutting all the smaller stuff to open up the area a little. Certain trees had a pronounced lean in one particular direction and had to be cut accordingly. With the dense growth of all the trees on this lot, an early problem we encountered was that the cut tree would start to fall, and then get hung up halfway down in the branches of a neighboring tree. So now we had to cut the second tree while keeping a watchful eye on the hung-up tree, or widow-maker, lest we get clobbered. Sometimes, a dead limb would snap off overhead without warning. To avoid serious injury, anyone who works in the woods must keep his wits about him at all times.

One time when we were clearing the property, we worked ourselves into quite a predicament. As we were cutting one tree down, it fell toward another and got hung up in the other tree's branches. So we tried cutting the second tree down and, as it began to fall, it too lodged into the crotch of a third tree. Things were looking very precarious with all three trees completely hung-up and leaning in various directions. As we carefully made the crucial cut at the base of the third tree, we listened for the telltale crack of the stump, quickly shut the chain saw off, and ran for cover. The three trees crashed to the ground around us, and we breathed a heavy sigh of relief. We needed a break to reconsider our game plan; there was no point in pushing our luck too far.

Brother Fred

I didn't really sign up for this detail, but somehow I got recruited. They asked if I could give 'em a hand clearing the land—a little chain sawing and burning of the brush. But you know how that goes—one thing leads to another, and pretty soon, it turns into a full-time occupation. I'll admit I have been getting a very thorough workout every day, every single muscle in my body. Clearing trees and working in the woods is certainly not for the faint-hearted. But this kind of work does make the beer taste awfully good after work.

Through July and August, my brother and I arrived at the property by 9:30 or 10:00 a.m. One of us would chain-saw and the other would stack firewood and clear branches. Usually by mid-afternoon, it was getting pretty hot and muggy, and we'd start running low on energy. The black flies and gnats were very annoying sometimes, but you just had to ignore them. The little stumps that stuck up from the ground several inches were murder on our ankles—you could hardly avoid tripping wherever you walked. Maneuvering a wheelbarrow full of wood through this minefield was very tricky business.

Every few hours, we would take a break. We'd usually sit on the ridge over on the north side of the property facing Canada and Lake Superior. Our T-shirts were soaked in summer sweat, and we were covered from head to toe with sawdust and pine needles. But a couple of ice-cold beers could sure take your mind off your troubles.

A few years ago, I helped my friend Ernie sell firewood. We drove his old Ford pickup out to state forest land, where he had a permit, and cut downed trees. We sawed them up, hauled them back to town, and split them with a maul and wedge. Talk about a great physical workout. But after all the expense of gassing up the truck and delivering cordwood to customers, we were lucky to break even. We didn't expect to get rich in the wood business, but I guess it kept us busy and out of trouble.

We had our share of close calls cutting trees. Some of these big maples and birches didn't always fall in the direction we expected; a heavy upper limb or the wind could make it swing one way or another. A few of those widow-makers that get hung up in the trees can flatten you in a heartbeat if you're not paying attention. And you also need to keep an eye out for those flying chains that, for some reason, come zipping off the saw now and then.

We spent over six weeks clearing off that property, and we were pretty whipped by the end. But I figured I had started this job, and I wanted to finish it. It was a heckuva workout. By the time the mosquitoes discovered us around six or seven each evening, we were about ready to call it a day.

After downing several good-sized maples or birches, we would spend the next couple of hours trimming off all the branches and cutting the trunk into sixteen-inch chunks for future firewood. Fred and I took turns on the chain saw while Judy and Brennan hauled the massive branches over to a pile to be chipped or burned later. Soon, so many stumps were sticking up that maneuvering a wheelbarrow full of wood was like running a downhill slalom. We seemed to trip, stumble, and curse every few steps.

Week after week, the brushing and clearing went on amid the summer heat, mosquitoes, and black flies. For the most part, the bugs left us alone each day until about seven in the evening, as if to remind us that it was time to quit for the day. It took a while to build up enough stamina to work in the woods all day long, especially in the sweltering humidity and intense heat. We took off work on Sundays and rainy days and occasionally an odd day here or there just to rest from the weariness and exhaustion. Working in the woods had strained muscle groups that we had long neglected, but little by little, our bodies grew taut and conditioned by the workload.

The lot was slowly opening up from the center outwards. We tried to save the most majestic trees on the property, many of the tall poplars and most of the stately maples. Gradually, we were able to visualize the layout of the long driveway leading up to the house near the back of the lot. We had to make sure we cleared enough trees to make room for the septic drain field as well as a front and back lawn. A well would still have to be drilled at least fifty feet from the drain field. Space for the two-car garage, which would be built a year later, also had to be accounted for. Progress was hard-earned that sweltering summer, but the once-overgrown lot was finally showing signs of a promising building site.

Judy

Oh, my God! Fred and Rich and I have been clearing the land for nearly six weeks now and I'm exhausted. They chainsaw the trees down and cut them up into short little pieces, and I wheelbarrow them over to the corner of the lot and stack them up in long rows. I think we've stacked about twenty face cords of firewood so far. My arms feel like wet laundry on a clothesline; my muscles are so sore. I hope this job builds character because, inch by inch, it is surely killing me.

And this place is so messy all the time. I go home with twigs and sawdust in my hair and underwear. It's just disgusting! Men don't seem to care how they look or smell. They just let it all hang out for what it's worth. But I've got a little pride in my appearance, you know. I don't go to the supermarket with my hair up in curlers, wearing a bathrobe, although I've seen people do that. What are they thinking?

But I'm not really one to complain. Take, for instance, all the firewood that I've wheel-barrowed around this lot all summer. It's not the wheel-barrowing that I mind so much. It's all those little stumps everywhere that I'm tripping over constantly, and the bending over and lifting and bending again and stacking of all this wood. I mean, do we really need this much fricking firewood? I sure hope it's all worth it in the end. Because these guys are working me like a slave. I'm a woman. Why should I have to do this kind of labor? Well, all right, I said that I wanted to be involved in this project, but it would be a little nicer if I could just choose which of the fun jobs I want to do. I'm not King Kong, you know.

After clearing the land for three or four weeks, we were nearing some of the larger trees on the lot's perimeter. As I mentioned earlier, anyone who has spent time in the woods with a chain saw knows that trees, when cut, don't always drop in the direction one expects. We ran into a situation once in which we had a very tall maple to cut near the east side of our property line. My neighbor's sixteen-foot boat and trailer rested innocently in the driveway next door, not more than thirty feet away. He was, unfortunately, gone for the day. Before starting the cut, we looked up at the heavier branches that might influence the fall's direction. The tree had a very slight southerly lean, but the heavier limbs were located on the easterly side. We could not afford to take even the slightest chance of dropping this humongous maple on my neighbor's driveway. If someone had been home that day, we would have asked to move the boat, just to be safe. That morning, three of us managed, using a thirty-two-foot ladder, to tie off a sturdy rope partway up the tree. The plan was that, as I made the final cut, Fred and Judy would pull on the rope for all they were worth in a southerly direction and drop it parallel to my neighbor's driveway.

The split second you make that final cut and hear the "crack" of the tree stump, the heavy tree will slowly begin to fall in a decisive direction. With the two of them straining hard on the rope, I made the last cut and heard the sharp "crack." Regretfully, we underestimated the weight of those upper limbs, and the falling maple lurched toward my neighbor's beautiful fiberglass speedboat. I yelled, "Pull! Pull hard!" As the towering tree fell eastward, it slammed hard to the ground with a deafening thud that took our breaths away. It had missed my neighbor's boat by a mere twelve inches. Without a doubt, my insurance company would not have covered the negligent destruction of a neighbor's property. I'm quite certain it doesn't insure against stupidity and foolishness. In fact, had it known, my insurance company might have considered dropping me as a client for being too much of a risk to its bottom line. Fortunately, I was saved the embarrassment of having to explain the matter to my new neighbor. Within thirty minutes, frantically sawing and trimming branches like madmen, we had removed from the crime scene every last trace of negligence and foul play.

Toward the end of August, we had piled half-a-dozen enormous stacks of brush around the property. Off to one side of the lot, we had also stacked over twenty-five cords of firewood for the cold winters ahead. To save time and to produce some landscaping material for future use, I rented a portable gas-powered wood chipper from our local hardware store. The store clerk claimed that this chipper was capable of handling trees and brush up to four inches in diameter. Fred and I figured it would take us about four or five good hours to shred these massive piles of boughs and branches.

Sadly, the dream machine was a dud from the very start, a colossal disappointment. This chipper bogged down with even the smallest twigs. It coughed, spit, groaned, and threatened to die every other minute. I think Popsicle sticks would have been too much for it. A two-inch diameter pine post had to be jammed into the noisy intake with constant hand pressure, but it could barely handle the force. We had thought that using a wood chipper would be like that powerful machine we had seen city workers use around town, tossing large branches into snarling chipper blades that, with an ear-splitting shriek, hungrily devoured their prey. Instead, our trusty machine whined, whimpered, and refused to obey. We hauled it ten miles back to town and moved on to Plan B.

The next morning, we returned to the site and burned the massive piles of foliage in an enormous bonfire. With the help of a couple of shots of garden hose connected to my neighbor's water supply, we were safely able to incinerate six weeks' worth of dried refuse. Joe and Deloris, Judy's mom and dad, came out to join us for a great end-of-summer picnic. We roasted hot dogs and marshmallows over the flames, washing them down with a few ice-cold Millers. This was the best way to end the long summer, we thought—with a bang, not a whimper. It beat running a chipper any day.

By early September, we had scheduled the excavator with his front-end loader to remove the stumps and reshape the contours of the building site. In clearing the land, we had tried diligently to save a few of the larger maples and birches in the middle of the site, thinking that they added a certain dignity to the landscape with their towering canopies. Only years later would we realize what an impractical idea that was. Trees are relatively easy to cut down when there is no house or garage on site to worry about. However, once buildings are in place, dropping a large tree safely and accurately requires great skill and a few prayers. When I returned from Traverse City a few days later, the excavator had removed all the stumps and buried them on the site's northeast corner. He had leveled out the uneven ground, and for the first time, we could actually visualize a grand log house on this property.

It was now mid-September, and the fall foliage had just begun its first act of breathtaking color spectacle. To the north, looking across the deep blue waters of the upper St. Mary's River toward Canada, we could see an occasional Great Lakes ore freighter making its way majestically downriver. The freighters were a cherished part of the perennial landscape, a way of measuring the passing of the seasons. It wasn't hard to imagine living in this idyllic location for the next twenty-five years.

We still owned our house in TC and traveled back and forth coordinating various subcontractors. I had purchased a rundown Dodge Caravan to help transport building materials. On most of my trips up to the Soo, my cocker spaniel Raleigh accompanied me. He was an English cocker with a long snout and good posture who strutted about like an aristocrat with a very dignified air, as if searching for his pipe and slippers. As he sat next to me in the van, looking so stately and watching the approaching traffic, it was as if he were thinking, "Carry on, my good man! Cheerio now. Everything appears to be on the up and up!" And then, with his monocle in place, he would return to reading his newspaper.

Raleigh usually came on these trips with me for a bit of adventure and quite often for the food. As soon as we neared Petoskey, he would abruptly sit up in the passenger seat with his nose held high in the air, sniffing. He never failed to catch the first whiff of the McDonald's drive-thru as we pulled up. I ordered two small cheeseburgers, one for Raleigh and one for me. Leaving his in the bag, I tossed it down on the floor of the van, and for the next hour, he was in hog heaven. He not only devoured the burger, but he chewed up most of the paper wrapper, leaving barely a trace of evidence. Raleigh was always good company on these trips and hardly ever complained about my conversation or my choice of music on the radio. A fine traveling companion, he was happy as long as we were on the road together, going somewhere. He managed to distract me from the never-ending stream of issues I was dealing with.

Before the excavator could begin digging the basement, a problem arose with the Chippewa County Health Department. When it had performed the mandatory soil tests, it had discovered a layer of hardpan about twelve inches below the ground surface. Hardpan is a dense, highly compacted combination of sand and clay that doesn't allow much water absorption. Therefore, the county was going to require us to add forty-eight inches of sand in order to install a safe and efficient septic field. This would be a considerable expense we hadn't foreseen.

Then, one day, when the excavator was digging the basement, he called me over to have a look at something. Under a ten-inch layer of hardpan, he had discovered nothing but pure sand. I quickly called the county official back to ask him whether he would come out and have a look, thinking this might save me the great expense of additional sand. If we could scrape away the layer of hardpan, we would have the perfect site that met all the health requirements. The official considered my proposal for a moment, then firmly decided against it because he thought the hardpan problem might still contaminate my neighbors' property in the future.

So we went ahead with the forty-eight inches of sand fill and, consequently, only had to dig down eighteen inches for the twelve-block-high basement walls. I was concerned that the house would appear to be sitting on top of a great mound, but eventually, once everything was leveled and landscaped, the house site looked quite proportionate with the contours of the adjacent land.

To save money, I had thought seriously about tackling the

basement-building project myself. Thank God, my designer/ builder Bob talked me out of it. Having built his share of basements over the years, he warned me that it would be more grueling and exhausting than I could ever imagine. The basement, he said, should be built by a professional with experience. As it turned out, that decision was money well-spent. Hauling cement blocks and mixing mortar for a large project is hard labor, pure and simple. Anyone who has ever done this kind of work will tell you it's not for amateurs.

By late September, the local builder we had subcontracted was pouring the basement footings. One of the main focal points of the house was to be a fieldstone fireplace, rising up some thirty-three feet from the basement. This was an enormous amount of weight that required a concrete pad measuring nine feet by seven with a thickness of one-and-a-half feet. The solid interior log wall that towered over twenty feet from the ground floor would need three cement pads measuring three feet square by one foot deep. The bearing weight of these two significant features was substantial, and the calculations could not be underestimated.

Gathering the round fieldstones for the fireplace steered us to several local gravel pits. My friend Ernie volunteered his pickup truck because my wimpy van would have bogged down quickly from the weight of stone. Fred, Ernie, and I sorted through pinkish, black, and striped "hardheads," trying to find a large number of smooth, colorful stones. We wanted to avoid the sedimentary sandstone because of its brittle character. Lining the box of his pickup truck with one layer of stone, we looked down at the truck's sagging springs. As we added about half a dozen more rocks, the springs suddenly snapped. We had pushed them a little too far.

On another rock scavenger hunt, Fred and I took our backpacks to an isolated stretch of beach on Lake Superior just west of town. We found some beautiful hardheads but could only carry a few at a time. Rock by precious rock, our pile began to grow.

From one of his many hiking expeditions on the Appalachian Trail, Fred had saved a very special rock to add to the fireplace. If you stared at this particular rock very intently, with the flickering shadows from a dying fire, you could make out a mysterious face like that of a cloaked druid. It helped, too, if you had downed a shot of whiskey beforehand. This special rock was placed in a prominent position near the fireplace's opening, waiting for a watchful eye and a wandering imagination.

The Big Day finally arrived on October 19th. It was a gorgeous, sunny fall morning as the three semi-trucks carrying our logs from Muskegon drove up the long dusty road to our site. The Maple Island log crew took over, and for the next three days, they hoisted these enormous logs, many as long as fifty feet, with an overhead crane, and swung them slowly into place. Once the walls had climbed to about four feet high, the crew took a break while the electrician drilled down through the solid log walls for his electrical wiring runs. This electrical work had to be done at certain stages of the wall construction, or the wiring couldn't be hidden from view.

When the log walls were being fitted and numbered in the Muskegon log yard months earlier, all the corner joints were saddle-notched and carefully fitted together. None of the window or door openings would be cut out until the logs arrived on the owner's site. The log builders measured and marked the locations of these future openings according to the blueprints. As the logs were maneuvered into position one by one, the crew would stack up three or four courses of logs before stopping to measure for the door and window openings. Four-foot long by half-inch thick iron rebar would then be hammered through a predrilled hole along both sides of each door and window opening. When the opening was later chain-sawed out, this iron rebar would help to keep the logs aligned until the new opening could be bucked, or reinforced, with two-by-eight lumber and eight-inch lag bolts. This was a crucial step in this style of log home construction. Any cutout opening without rebar would be vulnerable to partial collapse of the log wall.

Before the log walls started to go up, I had contacted a number of subcontractors familiar with the many peculiarities of log home construction. After they looked over the blueprints, we sat down and discussed the particular details of each job. Not all of the subs could be hired locally. The three carpenters who would install windows and exterior doors came from Traverse City. The installer of the stress-skin paneled roof system drove up from Midland.

The contracts we signed were fairly well-detailed and specified our agreed-upon prices and the work to be performed. Some of the carpentry work had to be open-ended and paid for on an hourly basis because many of the building tasks were to be delegated as needed. Certain jobs could only be completed if the weather were cooperative. Other work, like plumbing runs, could only take place when partition walls were installed. So, quite often, one subcontractor was waiting for the other guy to complete his share of the work before the next phase could begin. As Murphy's Law would have it, delays sometimes lasted for several weeks, bringing progress to a grinding halt.

I signed very specific contracts with the excavator, the plumber, the well-driller, and the masons. But the electrician was unable to nail down a set dollar amount because a lot depended on the exact lighting fixtures I would eventually choose, another task that we kicked a bit further down the road due to such a hectic schedule. He reassured me he could get the fixtures for me wholesale; unfortunately, I did not get that in writing—another mistake I would soon regret.

This being my first time acting as a general contractor, I neglected to cover certain details in the contracts we signed. There was no mention of any specific timetable for completing the jobs outlined and, more importantly, no monetary consequences for neglecting to finish the job in a timely manner. I assumed that subcontractors would realize that, with log home construction, not all jobs would proceed as quickly as with conventional construction. Inevitable delays would happen. But I didn't expect people under contract to delay me or bail out on me completely. Log home building seemed to bring with it a unique set of unforeseen problems and frustrations. Sorting them out would prove time-consuming and annoying for everyone involved.

After three intense days, the Maple Island log-setup crew finished its work, and the roofing phase began. It was nearly Halloween, and soon, the weather up north would take a turn for the worse. The carpenters raced to nail down over 2000 square feet of tongue-and-groove New Hampshire white-pine ceiling boards. They could not stand on the roof but straddled fifty-foot-long log purlins like Olympic gymnasts.

Before the carpenters could finish the roof, the sky darkened with black clouds, and the wind picked up speed. As a driving rain approached, I brought out a gigantic sixty-foot square tarp that I had purchased downstate for this very situation. We needed to stretch this humongous tarp over the roofline to protect the wood subfloor beneath as well as the pine roofing boards from being soaked. With eight of us scrambling to beat the storm, we tied twenty-foot ropes to every other grommet all the way around the tarp, which started to shake briskly in the rising wind. Like Lilliputians in *Gulliver's Travels*, we hustled and strained to tie the beast down before the full fury of the storm awoke. The large blue tarp flapped and twisted in the wind, but finally, it looked secure. The fall monsoon engulfed us, and there was nothing more we could do but take cover and wait.

When we returned the next morning, the skies had cleared. A light breeze blew in off the lake as we surveyed the debris of broken branches scattered about the yard. The damage had been done. Hanging raggedly from the roof, our enormous blue tarp had been ripped to shreds like a cheap T-shirt. Everything beneath the tarp was soaked through and through. Most of the metal grommets had been torn away by the gale's force. Obviously, we had lost that round. All we could do was swear a bloody streak to get it out of our systems. Then we picked up a couple of brooms and began sweeping the pools of water from the subfloor before everything was totally warped.

With so many subcontractors coming and going, I felt it was only reasonable that I provide them some sort of outdoor bathroom facility. Not wanting to pay for a porta-potty for months on end, I devised an alternative. Behind a small grove of spruce trees, off to the side of our lot, I set up a porcelain toilet that I had bought at a local yard sale. I mounted it on a plywood platform in the open air and stretched a small plastic bag over the rim of the toilet. Next to it was a five-gallon bucket filled with lime and a small scoop. The idea was to do your business and toss on a little lime and Presto!—a very simple, sanitary, and inexpensive operation. Only problem was that I became the one responsible for replacing the full bags, and most of the participants neglected to use lime, after all was said and done. It grew to be a very revolting line of work, but I couldn't very well ask anyone else to do the job

I had so ingeniously designed. It was a lesson well-learned about when to save money and when to shell it out. I knew for certain I had no practical future as a plumber.

While this was going on, work was progressing on other levels. The well was being drilled, the septic field was being laid out, and the carpenter from TC was busy cutting out the window and door openings. I watched as he studied the blueprints, measured over from a corner of the building, and marked the window opening on the logs with a black Magic Marker. He then skillfully chain-sawed one log at a time in the solid log wall. The opening was then bucked with two-by-eight lumber and lag-bolted to the logs through slots at the top and middle of the window opening. These slots allowed the logs to shrink as they dried and to settle vertically so the window would be undisturbed. The trim would later be nailed to the bucks rather than to the logs.

Everything was coming along fine until one day when the TC carpenter was almost finished cutting a good-sized opening for a set of exterior French doors. He had just completed the last cut and was preparing to buck the opening when he heard a sudden groan in the wall and saw that it was shifting slightly and possibly about to collapse on him. A twenty-two-foot-high solid log wall bears a tremendous amount of weight. Instantly, he sensed something very dangerous was about to happen, threw down his chain saw, and bailed out the side of the building along with his coworkers. The drop to the ground was about six feet since the outside deck had yet to be built. The logs in the door opening suddenly shifted out of alignment but did not buckle completely. Apparently, the log setup crew had somehow neglected to pound any iron rebar alongside the intended door opening as the log wall was being assembled. So there was very little to reinforce this opening once the log sections were cut out. Gravity is a powerful force, and this was a simple matter of physics. The entire wall could have collapsed within seconds.

The carpenters were quite shaken by this frantic moment and hesitant to go back inside the building. But, in time, they got up their courage and figured out a way, with large pipe clamps and jacks, to torque the logs back into alignment. They then screwed long lag bolts diagonally between the logs to strengthen the wall and finally, once the wall was straightened, they bucked the opening securely with two-by-eight lumber. This was only the first of many unexpected surprises that would come our way. It could have very easily become a disaster. We were off to a rather shaky start, and this time, we had just been lucky.

The Carpenter

The owner hired me and my two guys to come up from Traverse City to the Soo because we had experience working on log homes. Apparently, very few of the carpenters in the Soo area had ever worked with logs. Just as well because logs are dangerous, especially the bigger ones. This place has a lot of eighteen-inch butt diameter logs over fifty feet long; that's a helluva lot of weight.

I was hired to put in the windows and exterior doors before winter set in. On the blueprint, there are twenty-seven double-hung windows, three sets of French doors, two entrance doors, and three half-circle windows. Let me tell you, November in the U.P. is one helluva time to be putting in windows, let alone starting construction of a new house. But it's work, so we'll take it. My two helpers and I come up to the Soo for two or three days at a time and put in some long hours. It's damn cold and miserable up here in November with all the freezing rain and snow and frostbitten fingers. We stay in nearby motels in the evening and grab a bite at a local restaurant. We're just trying to work this job in with a few others back in TC.

Maybe you've already heard about the near calamity with the log wall almost collapsing on us. That log home crew forgot to insert the four-foot pieces of iron rebar in the right places so the walls could stay lined up. When that wall started groaning and began to shift, I got pretty nervous thinking it might all suddenly come crashing down. We abandoned ship in a heartbeat and didn't dare go back to work for nearly an hour.

So, you can see, building with logs is a tricky business. You've got to have your wits about you at all times. I didn't really mind the wall business that much; it's all part of the job, and it keeps me on my toes. But I think my two guys were scared shitless.

Meanwhile, before the roof could be shingled, stress-skin panels that had been custom-designed for our roof still needed to be assembled in place. Stress-skin panels are a state-of-the-art roofing system that, in theory, does not require any ventilation above it. The panels were constructed of half-inch-thick OSB (oriented strand board) on top and bottom that sandwiched an eight-inch thick layer of Styrofoam. By constructing them as large rectangles and triangles, the panels were designed to fit together to form a solid, super-insulated roof system. They were secured to the log purlins using twelve-inch-long screws.

The subcontractor we had hired to install these panels seemed to be making steady progress. But one afternoon, as I was working outside, I saw him up on the roof, lying motionlessly on his back, staring blankly at the sky.

"Hey! How's the work going?" I shouted up to him.

No answer, just a faraway look on his face.

"Are you having a problem? Can I help with anything?" I ventured again.

"Ah. I'm just frustrated. These panels aren't going together the way I'd like."

"Why not?"

I heard a low groan from him. "I can't say exactly, but these log homes always give me a headache. They are such a pain in the ass!"

I left him in peace for the moment, hopefully, to work out his frustrations. The next day, he didn't show up to work, even though the weather was cool and sunny. When I finished working that day and got back to town, I called him down in Midland, wondering whether he planned to complete the job. There was a long pause on the line, until finally he snapped:

"That's it! I've had enough! I'll never work on another log home again. Nothing ever fits right. I quit!"

As a subcontractor, he had signed an agreement to complete the work for a specific price, but, as I thought more about it, there was no point in suing the guy in court. Forcing him to complete the job might only lead to shoddy work, and I couldn't have that. He said he would give me a price break on the work that was completed so I could find another contractor. So we simply called it a day and moved on. There were too many other things to worry about with winter weather on the way.

The masons, meanwhile, were busy stacking up the cement block course by course for the fireplace. This massive structure arose from the basement floor, supported by a sturdy concrete foundation, and would ascend over thirty feet to the roof. Added to this masonry facade would be the carefully-crafted application of the individual fieldstones we had so painstakingly gathered from local gravel pits and lakeshores.

My friend Ernie helped the two masons mix mud in a wheelbarrow and transfer it to five-gallon buckets, which he carried up to the scaffolding along with a steady supply of sixteen-inch cement blocks. Ernie was used to working with concrete from his current job engraving and setting cemetery stones in graveyards. It takes a good deal of grit and a strong back to move cemetery stones around, a fact I discovered after helping him out a few times. The higher the fireplace walls grew, the higher Ernie had to carry the blocks and heavy pails of mixed cement up the ladder to the rising scaffolds.

"More mud! More block!" was all he heard that day.

I was out of town at the time, so he asked my brother Fred to help him the next day. Fred was reluctant, but Ernie pleaded: "No, you've got to help me. These guys are killing me with their 'More mud, more block bullshit.'" Fred finally agreed, and by the time I returned from TC, they had run the block almost to the ceiling. It reminded me of how grateful I was that Bob, who had helped us design the house plans, had talked me out of building my own basement. It really would have put me physically over the edge.

By early December that year, the snow was only a couple of inches deep as we began the precarious job of roof shingling. The house would have to be completely closed in very soon if we planned to work comfortably in it over the winter months. We had been fairly lucky that no major blizzards had blown through the Upper Peninsula so far. But the roof was icy and snow-covered, and climbing a forty-foot ladder with an eighty-pound bundle of shingles on your shoulder was no mean feat.

Along with my brother Fred, my brother-in-law Tom, and

his co-worker Tony, the four of us tackled the shingling job for several weeks leading up to Christmas Day. Tom and Tony worked together so often—sometimes one acted as the boss, sometimes the other—that we named them TNT Construction, an explosive pair of guys who knew how to get the job done.

A freezing wind was blowing up off the lake as we crawled on our knees across the roof. We hand-nailed the shingles, trying to keep all the rain lines straight. The tarpapered roof surface, dusted lightly with snow, made for slick footing in the cold morning air. We had snipped off the tips of our work gloves with scissors in order to hold the nails and, at the same time, keep our fingers warm.

Every couple of hours or so, we had to scramble down the ladders and dash inside to warm up a bit. Tom had brought over his propane Salamander to heat one of the cold cement-block rooms in the basement that we had designated our coffee room. We passed around a thermos of steaming coffee and a few Little Debbie cakes and watched the hissing blue-yellow flames shooting from the mouth of the Salamander. If anything could heat up a freezing room in a hurry, it was this machine. Tony took off his new thermal boots and put them near the heater to warm up. Hardly ten minutes had passed between the coffee and a few stories when Tony jumped to his feet and yelled.

"Holy crap! My boots!"

His new $150 thermal top-of-the-line boots had half-melted into a rubberized pile of goo. They looked like some abstract art object, faintly recognizable but hard to define. Tony was beside himself and swore like a man who'd lost his most prized possession. He had taken great pride in them and had worn them for only a week. Sadly enough for Tony, we had not paid much attention to the flaming Salamander's intense heat. Needless to say, he was not in a good mood the rest of the day. Somehow, we were able to finish the winter roofing job that afternoon, although Tony's frozen feet were never quite the same.

To hold the winter wind at bay, we hurried to plug the gaps by stapling strips of white Ethafoam between the logs. I had ordered large sheets of one-inch thick Ethafoam that I cut into various widths on my table saw in the basement. They needed a fifteen-degree angle on each side of the strip to fit the roundness of the logs. In the warmer spring weather, we would apply a quarter-inch thick layer of Perma-Chink over the foam, a meticulous job that would require many endless hours throughout the house.

Now that the windows and doors had been installed, the roof finished, and the cracks sealed with foam, we called for installation of the wood furnace in the basement. It could not be used until the chimney was run up through the roofline. The masons were waiting for a thaw in the weather, which usually comes a short time after Christmas. Running from one end of the house to the other, the fifty-foot-long ridge pole, measuring about sixteen inches in diameter at the roof's peak, would have to be chain-sawed through the middle section so the chimney could protrude. What pent-up tensions and stresses might suddenly be released when we made that final cut, we could not be certain. Beneath the roofline, we had permanently supported both sides of the ridge beam with adjustable stout posts.

On a balmy sunny day in January, with the mercury in the low forties and no wind, we knew we had only a small window of time in which to make the crucial cut through that beam and finish the masonry work. Straddling the roof's peak with a chain saw, having measured as accurately as possible for this potentially dangerous cut, I hesitated for a while, unsure of what might happen. Would the roof collapse? Would the ridge beam sag? I felt very nervous as the chain bit into the massive log, spitting coarse sawdust across the snowy roof. When it was over, nothing had moved, not even a millimeter. We had extracted a five-foot section of ridge beam with no repercussions. I felt such a sense of joy and relief that I slept like a baby that night.

The masonry work was scheduled to resume by 9:00 a.m. sharp the next morning. When Ernie arrived at 9:15 to help mix mortar and carry blocks, he unlocked the door to the house and found Huey the mason and his partner busily at work.

"How did you guys get in the house this morning?" Ernie asked since he had the only key.

"We climbed on the roof and shinnied down through the chimney," said Huey, deftly mudding another block into position. "If a man wants to get to work, he'll find a way."

Ernie could only shake his head in amazement.

"And by the way," Huey continued, tooling another mud joint, "work starts at 9:00 o'clock, not 9:15. Don't forget that."

The building was now completely sealed up for the winter weather, and we could now connect the wood furnace to the chimney to warm things up. We pitched half-a-dozen cords of firewood through the basement window and fired up the furnace for the first time. None of the ductwork to individual rooms was hooked up yet, so the heat had to rise from the basement and circulate on its own. Fifty-five to sixty degrees was a good temperature to work in; it was now warm enough inside to dry the stain, varnish, and fresh chinking.

Clyde Winberg, a local stone mason, came in next to apply the heavy round fieldstones to the outside of the concrete block chimney. The stones weighed ten to twenty pounds apiece and could only be mounted a foot in height per day. His skill and artistry were remarkable; he carefully placed and mudded each stone into position with such a masterly touch. To allow each layer of work enough time to dry and set up soundly, Clyde returned every two or three days until the work was completed. With today's high cost of heating a home for the winter, a traditional fireplace may not be the most practical choice to make; however, the fireplace Clyde built turned out to be one of the most striking features of this entire log house; it became the heart and soul of this home and would be well-used and enjoyed for many years to come.

Chapter 5

Shelter

First we shape our buildings, and thereafter our buildings shape us.
— **Winston Churchill**

The era of miners, lumberjacks, and farmers in the U.P. over the last two hundred years has significantly influenced the design of many homes and other structures. In early nineteenth century America, as New England families moved further west, they brought along the heritage of the eastern states. Due to the difficulties of building in a new region of the country, often wilderness, many of the early homes in Michigan were quite modest—rough-hewn log homes or board shanty houses.[5]

After copper was discovered in the Keweenaw Peninsula, many Calumet miners who lived in the Upper Peninsula during the late nineteenth century lived in modest homes built by the mining company. "The C & H Company [Calumet and Hecla Mining Company] built some 1,200 homes for its workers . . . . Many of the houses were two-and-a-half stories and shingle-sided, built on rock formations made of mine debris."[6] It was difficult to afford much on miners' wages, and the miners' homes reflected that reality in their simple and stoic design.

Until the 1830s, most buildings in America were assembled

with post-and-beam frames by craftsmen using mortise-and-tenon joints.[7] About this time, "balloon framing" was invented, a development that would change the mechanics of home construction forever. History shows that:

> modern American house construction probably began in the fall of 1832, when a man named George Snow built a warehouse in Chicago . . . . He put his warehouse together with lumber that, compared to New England's posts and beams, resembled sticks. He assembled the frame with the ancestors of the dimension-stock two-by-four. He placed those sticks close together, making many thin pieces of wood take the place of a few hefty timbers, and fastening the pieces to each other with nails.[8]

This so-called stick construction came to be known as balloon framing. "It would never have developed if not for the invention of the steam-powered sawmill (which ensured a ready supply of lumber of consistent dimensions) and manufactured nails."[9] Mass production of nails had begun about thirty years earlier, so they were relatively cheap and plentiful by the time balloon framing came along. The economics of this innovation had a significant impact. Stick construction "reduced, by roughly half, the total volume of wood needed for a sturdy frame. A balloon frame could be made more quickly and erected with fewer hands than a frame of posts and beams."[10]

On the other hand, we have to give a firm nod toward the durability of post-and-beam construction. Many weathered barns across the Upper Peninsula and elsewhere have stood the test of time because of their superb craftsmanship and massive dimensions. Winter blizzards and gale-force winds have been unable to put a dent in many of these old buildings. The mortise-and-tenon joints that were painstakingly fitted together and pinned with wooden pegs have proven their worth over the years. As a result, modern timber framing has undergone a resurgence of popularity in the past several decades as a form of homebuilding in which the aesthetics of craftsmanship play a major role. Far fewer carpenters currently available are skilled enough to cut and fit together joints of this scale and to lift and position the massive beams into place. Despite the higher costs involved with timber framing, this construction style still enjoys a strong appeal in many regions.

In the 1800s, several developments drove people to settle in Michigan's Upper Peninsula. The abundant lumber in its vast forests, major mineral discoveries, and farming opportunities—all these factors combined to spur the settlement of this wild and primitive land. "From 1840 to 1850, the population of the Upper Peninsula grew sharply from thirteen hundred to almost six thousand."[11] There was a sense of grand adventure for those moving westward into unexplored territories.

In 1844, iron ore was first discovered in present day Negaunee, Michigan. This discovery "gave birth to the iron industry of the Lake Superior region."[12] In the early 1840s, massive quantities of copper were discovered in the U.P.'s Keweenaw Peninsula.[13] As iron ore mines multiplied, shipping on Lake Superior soared. Great fortunes were waiting to be made by aspiring entrepreneurs in this vast land rich in lumber and mineral deposits.

By 1855, the first State Locks, as they were called, and shipping canal were opened in Sault Ste. Marie to accommodate the tremendous increase in shipping traffic to and from Lake Superior.[14] Up to this time, ships had to be unloaded at the Soo, portaged a great distance, and reloaded before continuing their journeys—a costly and time-consuming undertaking. This new lock significantly reduced the time and expense of transporting goods on the Great Lakes.

Despite the wealth of growing opportunities in Michigan's Upper Peninsula, mining companies "complained how hard it was finding men willing to work in the rugged wilderness of the Lake Superior region."[15] Workers were afraid of freezing to death in the bitterly cold region. They would have no problem staying warm with the plentiful supply of wood in the surrounding forest. However, "Food was another story . . . . The pioneer settlers had to rely almost solely on provisions shipped in during the preceding summer or fall. These stores had to last during the long months when navigation on Lake Superior was impossible. If the last boat with winter supplies failed to arrive, starvation would follow."[16] Without question, a timid soul would not survive in this harsh climate.

When iron ore was discovered in Negaunee in the mid-nineteenth century:

> a great number of Finns, Germans, and Swedes moved to that area for jobs in the mining industry. Due to many bleak winters in their native Finland, the various wars fought with Russia, and the overall inhospitable climate, the Finns developed strength of will and perseverance that is known today as *sisu*. Some say it means determination or decisiveness to get things done against impossible odds. Others say it's just pigheaded stubbornness.[17]

Whatever the case may be, I feel blessed that I have inherited enough *sisu* from my ancestors to give me the strength to get through difficult times without complaint.

In the late 1800s, my great-grandfather, Gust Hill, came to the U.P. from Finland and settled his family in the Ishpeming area. His son, William Hill, became the mining inspector at the Barnes-Hecker ore mine, which collapsed in 1926, a tragedy that killed fifty-one miners, including William. His son, Norman, who was twelve years old at the time, grew up without a father. During the Depression years, he worked at one of the Civilian Conservation Camps (CCC) in the Upper Peninsula, and then relocated to the Soo area for employment.

About this time, Mary Powell, a young girl who had moved to the Soo with her family from a farm outside of Toronto, was waitressing at the Harris Café. Here she met Norman and, within a few years, was married to him. Not long after the Pearl Harbor attack, he joined the U.S. Army and fought during World War II in France and Italy. After he returned home to Michigan, the two of them raised a family of five children—four boys and a girl—of which I am the youngest.

The reason I relate all these personal family details is simply to establish my U.P. Finnish heritage and to help explain what influences my background may have had on my own attitudes and personal beliefs. The serendipity and random circumstances of one's past, small decisions that lead down one path rather than another, combine to make each of us who we are today. Having grown up under modest economic conditions, each of us learned to appreciate what we had and to respect the value of a dollar. Money was never easy to come by, and we learned to be thrifty and wise spending it. The sub-zero temperatures and heavy snows of long U.P. winters tempered us in ways that would help us withstand other unexpected difficulties down the road. Our family background and our geographical environment went a long way in determining who we are.

Many of the Finns who settled in the U.P. during the late 1800s were known to be good carpenters and shipbuilders. These skills would prove to be essential as this heavily wooded region was being settled. "Most of the Finns came to the Middle West and worked in the mines and forests and later on the land."[18] They were quite familiar with the grit and toil of a hard day's work and labored to support their growing families. Even in the mine, "work . . . not only was back breaking but dangerous. Accidents were common and men were killed almost daily. Other mines were so wet that miners lost their health. Many died of silicosis, miner's consumption. Explosions occurred often, killing many. Others drowned when the mine was flooded."[19]

The mines weren't the only dangerous place to work in the U.P. The lumberjacks of the north woods faced grueling, backbreaking labor on a daily basis. But they seemed to take it all in stride. To them, "hardship meant little or nothing."[20] They expected to work hard in the woods and weren't disappointed. As a typical lumberjack would proudly say, "[W]e faced the future with boundless optimism and faith in ourselves to handle any situation."[21]

If you were a lumberjack, work was plentiful in the Northern Michigan woods. The men were well fed but worked long hours from daylight to dusk. Following the seasonal changes, "men went to the woods in the fall and stayed until the camps broke up in the spring."[22] The logging operation continued year round. In the fall and winter, the timber was cut and skidded to nearby lakes and rivers; then, in the spring, the logs were driven down the rivers to the sawmills to be cut into lumber.

Many of the often-told stories of drunken lumberjacks in the woods have been overstated. In reality, the logging camp bosses and the men themselves would never have put up with anyone drinking on the job because "whiskey didn't mix with double-bitted axes, crosscut saws, falling trees, widow-makers, icy roads, log jammers, and river driving."[23] Work in the woods was too dangerous to have anyone around who was not sober and alert.

With such a hearty and physically demanding way of life, the U.P. lumberjack became known for his fierce independence and self-reliance. By the early 1950s, the lumberjack era was fading fast. "The saga of the old-time lumberjack in the woods and the whitewater man on the rivers is practically over. It lasted almost one hundred years."[24] From such colorful and hard-working ancestors, the U.P. character has been marked and imprinted, an influence that is still felt today in our attitudes and beliefs.

As our dream of someday building a log home in the U.P. gradually took root, our awareness of U.P. history—of lumberjacks, miners, and the building of rustic log shelters in the north woods—played an important role. The choice of massive red pine logs from the Michigan forest to construct a home seemed like the most natural option for a setting in the U.P. woods. Logs would certainly last as long as post-and-beam construction. A sturdily-built log home would suggest the integrity and timelessness of a well-built U.P. barn. If cared for and maintained, nothing would ever destroy it. The house could be our legacy for generations to come. So, in some small way, we would be leaving behind a human footprint in time.

For hundreds of years, people across the U.P. have heated their homes with wood and many still do today. As lumber was harvested and people cleared the land to create farms, wood as a fuel was always plentiful. Sawmills created an extensive supply of leftover slab wood in their operations, both hardwood and softwood, that was often used to heat homes and businesses. Across America, at one time, wood was a prime source of fuel. "As late as 1859, 90% of the national heating requirement was met by burning wood."[25]

Wood as a resource was also in strong demand for furniture making, transportation, and shipbuilding. "In the cities . . . many of the tradesmen were primarily woodworkers: the wheelwright, the cabinetmaker, the cooper, the shipwright, the carpenter, the carver. And as the nation grew, depending on wood for its very survival, the local supply of easily available fuel wood became threatened."[26] In the north woods of Michigan, as well as other regions of the country, it may have seemed like there was such an endless supply of lumber that logging companies felt free to clear-cut many of the great stands of primary forest. "The consequences were inevitable. By the late 1800s the prime forests of New England had been lumbered off, and then across the Northeast to the Great Lakes and on . . . ."[27]

By the twentieth century, we began to use forest resources in a different way. As a result, "fossil fuels replaced wood as a source of heat and power. As we learned how to use the trees of prehistoric times, the woodbox was replaced first by the coalbin and then by the oil barrel . . . it may have prevented catastrophe in the forests."[28] Our dependence on fossil fuels is a problematic issue in itself with regard to environmental pollution and the use of a rapidly disappearing resource. The threat to our forests has been greatly diminished through the use of selective cutting practices and good forest management.

In the early days of building shelters across America, a number of superstitions developed. The design of doors, for example, often had a religious connotation. "A godly man might prefer a Christian door with stiles (vertical pieces) and rails (horizontal pieces) that formed a Christian cross. A superstitious person might put a Maltese cross in the lower section and thereby make a 'witch door' to keep out the evil spirits . . . ."[29] They took pride in their craftsmanship, but especially in the design of their doors. The abundance of wood helped early builders to express themselves in a way that no other material would allow. Over the years, it has clearly been shown that "man has an affinity with wood not only as a mere material, but also as a kindred spirit to live with and to know."[30] The Michigan north woods offered the early settlers not only a means of making a living for their families but also a valuable resource for expressing themselves through the design and construction of their shelters.

Another common practice, especially in New England, was to nail an evergreen bough or small sapling to the ridge of a newly framed roof and drink a toast. "The conifer is thought to imbue the frame with the tree spirit, or it's meant to sanctify the home, or to appease the gods for the taking of the trees that went into the frame."[31] This ritual was referred to as "wetting the bush." Today, when people build or buy a new house, they usually celebrate by throwing a house-warming party. Friends bring gifts and food offerings to wish them well in their new lives and to drink a toast for good luck.

Since the early pioneer days, Americans have prided themselves on the virtues of self-reliance and perseverance. The same could be said for those first settlers and adventurers who came to the Upper Peninsula of Michigan in the early 1800s to seek their fortunes. There were no roads or bridges, nor any infrastructure like we have today, no electricity or indoor plumbing, no gas-powered vehicles or Internet. They made do with what they had and devised solutions from the resources available. Using horses and wagons and crude tools such as axes, come-alongs, and crosscut saws, these brave men and women were determined to carve out an existence in the densely-wooded forests of Upper Michigan.

As I look back at the roots of my family's desire to build a log home in the U.P., I recall those who came before me, knowing the importance of harsh weather and environment in molding the people who live here. We have benefited immensely from the efforts, ideas, and progress of our ancestors whose hard work provided the backbone of the lives we enjoy today. Learning to live in the U.P., over the course of many trying years, its people have through necessity developed many useful survival skills—psychological, physical, and economic—to get them through hardship and difficult times. The long winters are often brutal, stretching from November to April, so they put one's resolve firmly to the test.

Yoopers (as U.P. residents are known) often rely on more than one source of employment to make it through the year. Many hunt and fish for sport as well as a means of bringing in food. Wearing heavy down parkas and insulated boots, splitting firewood, shoveling roofs and driveways, driving on icy roads—these are all part of the mix of living up north. Overcrowding is certainly not a problem in the Upper Peninsula. With over 16,000 square miles of land area and a population of approximately 310,000 people, the U.P. averages about nineteen people per square mile. Social amenities and cultural offerings are more limited than in many of the cities below the bridge. However, no shortage of activities exists for those who like to skate, ski, or snowshoe in the winter and camp, boat, or hike in the summer. And yet, living in this harsh environment, one learns to appreciate the quiet beauty of an area that is not overwhelmed by the developments of man and machines.

It seems that many of us, usually when we're young, have

both a yearning to leave home, to strike out on our own and explore the world, as well as a strong urge to return home many years later, perhaps to rekindle something we lost along the way. This mysterious impulse to come back to our roots exerted a pull on Judy and me that was difficult for us to understand. Perhaps we wanted to leave a more difficult life behind and find a simpler pace of living. My personal reasons for coming back were clear: to be closer to family as we started to raise our own children. They would have the advantage of growing up, surrounded by grandparents as well as uncles, aunts, and cousins. Also, by living in the U.P., many outdoor activities such as camping, cross-country skiing, and fishing would, almost literally, be right out our back door.

For most of my life, I had always harbored the ambition to become a carpenter or woodworker. Having worked in retail businesses for nearly ten years, I yearned to get back to working on something more tangible—why not a house? Back in college, I had designed and built furniture pieces and really enjoyed the hands-on approach to working with tools and wood. I'd had the good fortune of studying the work and ideas of master furniture-builders like James Krenov, Wendell Castle, Sam Maloof, and George Nakashima—all highly-skilled craftsmen who stretched the concept of furniture from utilitarian to purely sculptural. What one could do with wood was unlimited. Furniture-making somehow seemed to ground me and connect me to the world in a way that business pursuits never could. Woodworking was tangible proof that by making daily progress in the design and building of a piece of furniture, though it was slow and methodical, I could achieve a finished result whose craftsmanship I was proud of. Gradually, I began to sense a strong identification and desire to become more self-sufficient and independent. My cultural roots seemed to be taking hold, driving us in a challenging and sure-footed direction.

When Henry David Thoreau built his small cabin on Walden Pond back in 1845, he was searching for a new self and a new life. It was a humble undertaking, but for him, it represented a chance to boil life down to its most basic elements. Thoreau encouraged each of us to take chances in life: "If one advances confidently in the direction of his dreams, and endeavors to live the life which he has imagined, he will meet with a success unexpected in common hours."[32] In the design of his simple hut, he included only what he needed and no more. For him, it was important to confront life at its most essential level. He was eager to learn whatever life could teach him.

When we construct homes today, many of us over-design and over-build, creating rooms that will hardly ever be used and spaces whose size overwhelms us. They seem to be structures built to impress one's neighbors rather than livable spaces created to harmonize with one's personal lifestyle. As a result, many homes appear cold and sterile, more like museums than personal living spaces. As Sarah Susanka, in *The Not So Big House*, gently reminds us: "We are all searching for home, but we are trying to find it by building more rooms and more space. Instead of thinking about the quality of the spaces we live in, we tend to focus on quantity. But a house is so much more than its size and volume, neither of which has anything to do with comfort."[33]

Earlier homes in the U.P. were built with the utmost practical considerations—a shelter to protect one from the elements, a place to cook and store one's provisions, a place to sleep. Today, a home must meet those minimal requirements and go far beyond. The design and aesthetics of a house play an essential role in creating a pleasing environment in which one wants to spend his free time. Choice of materials makes an important difference also—from ceramic tile and hardwood floors to granite countertops and quality lighting fixtures. Furnishings need not be ostentatious; sometimes, simpler is better, and less is more. Many people today are building much smaller homes but designing them with a greater sense of aesthetics and practical function.

In some ways, as we designed our log house, it was a blessing to have such a limited budget to work with. This prevented us from spending too much on frivolous features that could not prove their worth. We wanted the overall layout to appear bold and striking, yet somewhat modest and practical. Showy and ostentatious features never appealed to either of us. The main focus would be on the home's craftsmanship and details, on quality rather than quantity. If we were to accomplish our true goal, it would require persistence and resourcefulness, with a steady eye on the dream. In many ways, Thoreau's simplicity and directness would serve as our touchstone.

South side elevation

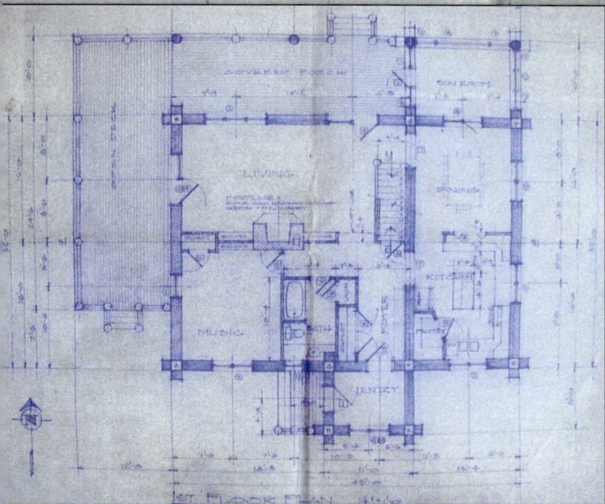

1st floor plans

2nd floor plans

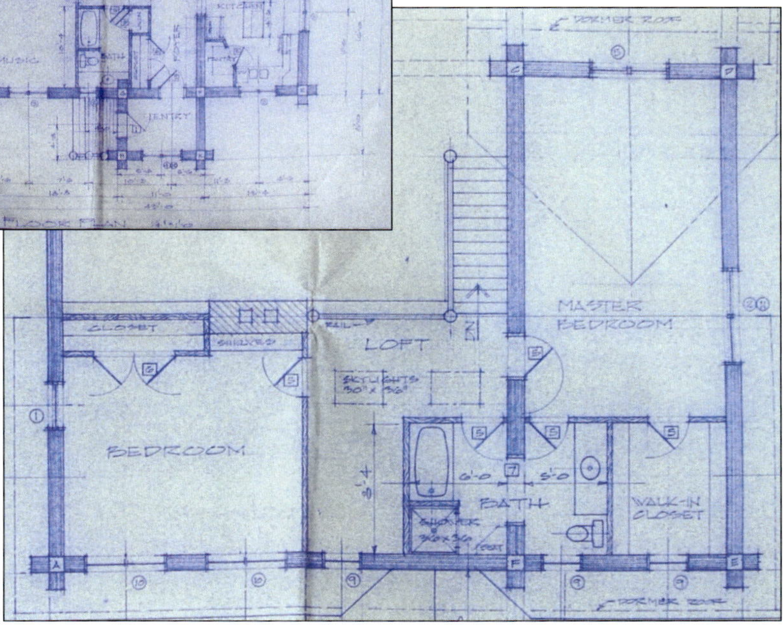

Forever Yours, Cherryland Mall

Clearing the lot

Brennan, wheel barrowing

Brennan, burning brush

Joe and Deloris, helping out

Rich, clearing the lot

Celebrating progress

Cement poured for foundation and pads

Smoothing the basement floor

Framing the main floor

Maple Island crane

Pounding rebar to reinforce log alignment

Northeast view of roof purlins

Interior west wall

Applying tongue-and-groove ceiling boards

Winter setting in; 1st floor windows installed

Stress-skin roof panels

Raising roof panels

Southwest view of building

Future kitchen before window openings are cut

Tom and Tony amid winter construction

Judy, stacking fireplace blocks

Shingling back porch

Shingling roof, December 1990: Fred, Rich, Tom, and Tony

Warming up in basement from winter roofing

U.P. shelter, example of early log construction

Travis, going fishing

Clyde, mudding stones for fireplace

Early stages of fieldstone application

Fieldstone fireplace with log mantle installed

Ernie, mixing cement for blocks

Masons mudding chimney blocks during January thaw

Cutting log support beam intersecting with fireplace; notice adjustable support posts

Master bedroom closet wall;
note space at top of stud wall to allow for settling

Kitchen corner before attaching plywood panels and hickory cabinets

Kitchen wall notching for two-by-four studs

Coleman, sweeping up kitchen sawdust

Installing kitchen cabinets

Setting kitchen ceramic tile

Judy, reloading chinking gun

Fred, chinking upstairs bedroom

Judy, stuffing fiberglass insulation in cracks

Balancing act to grind ridgepole

Fred, installing flooring

Flooring the master bedroom

Raising the log stairway into position

The boys' bedroom; notice adjustable jack under log post

Southeast view of house

Back porch after a winter storm

After February blizzard

Afternoon break in the woods

Chapter 6

Branching Out

We are made to persist.
That's how we find out who we are.
— **Tobias Wolff**, *In Pharaoh's Army*

As the winter of 1990-91 ushered in below-zero nights and bone-chilling blizzards, we had sealed up the log house enough to hold a small measure of heat. It was early February, and the ice on our bay had thickened to the point where fishermen felt safe hauling their tarpaper shacks across the frozen surface with snowmobiles. The chinking and the inside foam-stripping between logs had not been completed yet, so the wind that blew in off the lake could, in many places, still whistle through the logs. The wood furnace in the basement kicked out enough BTUs to take the chill out of the air, but we were still waiting for the ductwork to the upper floors to be installed. To keep our hands warm so we could work inside, we goosed the room temperature with a small propane heater.

The windows and exterior doors had been installed by the TC carpenter, who had returned home by this time. My wife noticed that the dining room and kitchen double-hung windows looked a little cockeyed, so we put a level up to them. They were so far out of plumb that we had to remove them completely to straighten up the framework and reinstall them. This would not be the last time we would have to redo someone else's work that we had already paid for.

I had created a lengthy punch list of jobs that needed to be completed next. There was no second floor to stand on yet besides the log joists, so my brother Fred and I tackled that job. We used two-by-six tongue-and-groove pine lumber to construct both the ceiling of the first story and the floor for the second. It was about forty degrees inside, which is comfortable as long as you keep working. When the basement wood furnace was fired up on cold winter days, we would wait for the red-hot coals to accumulate and place a couple of foil-wrapped pasties in the bottom. There is nothing like a steaming hot pasty to comfort you on a cold winter's day. We could appreciate the goodness and warmth my Finnish ancestors must have felt when they lunched on pasties and tea down in the mines many years ago.

Most of the log surfaces inside had major chatter marks from the debarking machines that had been used to strip the logs. We couldn't very well just stain and varnish over such a rough surface even though the log company maintained that most people preferred the "rustic" look. So I purchased a heavy duty Milwaukee auto body grinder to sand down the interior logs. It was exhausting and very dusty work, but Fred and I took turns with the grinder, which weighed close to twenty pounds, and sanded down every square inch of the interior log walls. To avoid breathing the heavy cloud of dust that formed, we both wore dust masks and goggles. It took the better part of two weeks to complete the entire grinding job. By the time we had finished and swept and vacuumed up the wood dust, we had filled over thirty large plastic garbage bags, having inhaled more than our fair share. It was likely the worst, most disgusting, grunt job of the entire process, but there was no getting away from it. Once that job was over with and the dust had cleared, we could start bleaching the logs.

As the moisture in the logs slowly dried out, the most mysterious looking forms of mold appeared at various locations. Some looked like mushroom fungus or cottage cheese; others took on a black powdery form that disintegrated like delicate crystal when you touched it. By bleaching the logs, we could brighten them as well as arrest any lingering mold within. We usually mixed the chlorine bleach fifty-fifty with water and loaded up the ten-gallon sprayer. Despite goggles and a breathing mask, the bleaching fumes still got into our lungs and made us go into coughing fits. We stopped regularly to open the windows for fresh air. At one point, I noticed that the bleach had dripped down past my rubber gloves and eaten into my wrist a hole the size of a nickel. We couldn't finish this phase of the operation fast enough.

Once the bleached logs had dried out, Fred and I began staining and varnishing all the interior log surfaces. The furnace had to be fired up to the max so the finish could dry properly. Next, the Ethafoam strips were stapled in place between the logs for insulation and to act as a backer for the chinking. By springtime, we were ready to begin the interior chinking. We had started off with about a dozen five-gallon buckets of Perma-Chink, a light gray latex-based product that had the consistency of mashed potatoes. In about a week's time, the gooey chinking would dry to a rubbery yet flexible state that would adhere to the logs as they shrunk. This was a job we had truly underestimated. Anyone can chink, but if you want to do a professional job, you have to gain some experience and work very patiently. Using a large stainless-steel chinking gun, you suck the chink out of a five-gallon bucket by pulling back on the plunger. It requires some upper body strength and a couple of loud groans to get it done right.

Sometimes, we could hear Judy down in the basement reloading her chinking gun, straining every muscle: "Ahhhhhhhh . . . Jeeesus! Ahhhhhh . . . Jeeeesus!" (And that from a girl who was once a good Catholic.)

After applying the chink, you squirt it with a few sprays of water, then carefully tool it to about a quarter-inch thickness, using several sizes of flexible putty knives. You spray the chink line a little more so the tools don't stick to it, and using lots of rags or paper towels, you wipe the cascade of gray drips as they continuously run down the logs. It's a very messy, sticky operation that takes a lot of practice to improve and also ruins whatever sweatshirt or blue jeans you happen to be wearing. The gray latex chink dries on your clothes permanently and stubbornly refuses to come out in the wash. Getting it out of your hair might require a pair of scissors.

Before too long, it became obvious to me that we would need to invest in some specialized tools to complete certain jobs. Besides the chain saw and the auto body grinder, we purchased a twelve-inch thickness planer to do trim work, a portable chop saw for carpentry, and a variety of hand tools for tiling and plumbing jobs. By doing most of the labor ourselves, we figured we saved enough to invest in some practical, well-made tools. If there was a job we weren't quite sure how to tackle properly, we purchased how-to manuals and read up on it. I soon developed a small library of books on plumbing, tiling, dry walling, flooring, and so forth. If the job felt too dangerous or too complex, we would hire it out through a subcontractor.

After the interior log walls were stained, varnished, and chinked, we could begin construction on the partition walls. These were built using two-by-fours, but they could not be attached to the logs in a conventional way. Where a two-by-four meets a log wall, it was necessary first to chain-saw and chisel out enough of the logs so the lumber could join the wall flush. Slots also had to be chiseled out near the top and middle of that two-by-four into which six-inch lag bolts with washers would fit. This procedure would allow the logs that adjoined the partition wall to shrink and settle as they slowly dried out. A great deal of log movement occurs in the first couple of years, and provision must be made for the settling that will take place above all windows and doors, as well as above and beside partition walls. Where a partition wall meets the ceiling, you must allow at least three inches for settling; otherwise, the wall gets crushed over time. Lag bolts attach to the ceiling through the top plate of the partition wall and help to stabilize the wall as the rest of the building shrinks. Trim is nailed only near the top and covers the gap at the top of the wall. It's all very time-consuming, labor-intensive business. Building with logs is like juggling live chain saws—if you don't pay close attention to details, there will be hell to pay.

Hanging kitchen cabinets on a log wall follows a similar procedure. Eight-foot two-by-fours are positioned vertically every twenty-four inches on the kitchen wall. The wall is then chain-sawed so the two-by-fours fit flush into the logs and, at the same time, form a flat plane. Each is slotted at the tops and middle for lag screws. To this surface, sheets of three-quarter inch plywood are screwed to form a solid, plumb surface for attaching wall cabinets that will stand the test of time. Again, this procedure is quite labor-intensive but absolutely necessary to allow the log wall to settle independently behind the cabinets.

Plumbing and electrical installation also have to take into account the movement of the log walls. This concern no doubt drives some of the subcontractors a little crazy; logs are somewhat of an unknown and unpredictable factor. As they shrink, sometimes they settle; other times, they twist, causing more than a few challenging problems. We had to install adjustable jacks in the walls on both sides of the masonry chimney in order to drop the floor level and the height of the ridgepole in the roof. Every few months, we lowered the height a small amount to account for the overall shrinkage in the outside log walls. In the same way, we trimmed the vertical log posts on our back porch each year to allow the roof to settle with the rest of the building. It may sound like a lot of tweaking and adjusting, but it never took very long to do once everything was in place. Day by day, we were learning new things, gaining confidence, and slowly adapting to this strange beast's peculiarities.

The Plumber

I've been hired to run the pipes in this log home, which, at first, is no big deal. The basement layout is pretty simple stuff. But once you get up to the first and second floors, everything gets a little hairier. Log walls move as they dry out, so I have to work that into my pipe layouts. It drives me a little bonkers. To tell you the truth—I really can't stand doing these log homes—too many damn problems to worry about.

I would prefer the standard two-by-four construction of conventional houses instead of this bullshit. Why didn't they just build a nice bi-level or Colonial? So much less hassle for everybody. I'm the kind of guy who likes to do his job, go home, and have dinner and maybe a couple of beers. I don't want to lay awake at night thinking about the pipe layout of this log home and whether or not it will spring a leak. I don't want to have to come back to redo a ruptured pipe because the logs settled too much.

Not only that. This customer makes me wait. He says the inside walls won't be ready until he finishes laying out the plumbing wall for the second-floor bathroom. He's trying to save a buck by doing most of the work himself, but he's holding me up. You can't build a log house on a shoestring budget, but he's trying, let me tell you. I may have to wait several months before I can finish up my end of this job. Like I said, I hate working on log homes. This is the last time I put up with such BS. A guy can't make any money like this.

By mid-June, the warm days of summer had finally returned and we started work on the house's exterior. We applied several coats of Lifeline finish to the logs, and then returned to the chinking job, which seemed to take forever. On sunny days, we spent so much time crawling up and down ladders that we began to develop "monkey feet," a term we used to describe the way our feet wrapped around the ladder's rungs when we wore soft-soled tennis shoes. The outside window trim was next and required more chain-sawing and chiseling to align the trim with the various thicknesses of logs. We made a cardboard template for the half-round window trim and pieced the parts together. After a great deal of fitting and grinding, the half-round trim went together nicely. It was very slow going, but that's what good craftsmanship requires: great care and patience.

The ever-present punch list grew longer every day; we'd finish two jobs and add three more. There were over 150 log ends on the exterior corners, and each log end had to be ground down at a forty-five-degree bevel with the auto body grinder. Holding that machine over your head for several hours, while standing on a sixteen-foot aluminum ladder, was a test of will and upper-body endurance. I had tried using a lighter weight drill with a small sanding disc, but it was much too wimpy and did a poor job. The Milwaukee grinder, monster that it was, had proven itself.

As summer progressed, we subcontracted a few of the other jobs. There were four roof-mounted skylights to be installed and aligned accurately between the roof purlins while cutting through twelve inches of stress-skin paneled roof—not a job for the young and inexperienced. Any errors here would be too costly. We also hired another local craftsman to custom-build three eight-foot bookcases with lower doors and install them in the living room and office. The summer months seemed to be flying by, so we hired Tom and Tony (TNT) to build a sixteen-foot by thirty-two-foot deck before the warm weather was gone. Slowly, we whittled down our long punch list of jobs, and we managed to maintain a high level of craftsmanship in our work, but everything was taking twice as much time as expected. We needed to find a way to speed things up. I wouldn't compare our project to that of slaves working on the Great Pyramids of Egypt. But the thought crossed my mind.

The Electrician

Not everyone agrees with me, but I'm not afraid to speak my mind. I've been in this business long enough to know the ropes, and I don't really care what people say about me as long as I get paid on time. Some of these general contractors I work for wait forever sometimes to pay me, like I don't have bills of my own to pay. Who do they think they are? Anyway, I do good work, and I'd like to get paid for it if that isn't asking too much.

This guy building the log home out west of the Soo calls me and wants an estimate on the electrical work. So I look over the blueprints and give him my best estimate based on a certain number of hours. You can't really tell with these log homes because you have to hide wires between logs, chisel out switch and outlet boxes, and allow for the settling of the logs. It all takes more time than regular construction. This guy's trying to get me to give him a dirt-cheap estimate, but I'm not working for peanuts. He says he will hang all the light fixtures if I will just locate the various switch boxes and hang the wire out from them. That's fine with me. And he can chisel out the boxes while he's at it, too.

Last week, I sent the owner my first bill, since I plan on billing every couple of weeks. He was real upset over my portal-to-portal charges on the bill. In other words, I charge a customer my hourly rate from the moment I climb into my truck until I arrive at the job site. In this case, it's about a forty-five-mile drive. That's work time to me. He doesn't think he should have to pay me for this, but that's how I make my living. Tough shit if he doesn't like it. Hire someone else; I don't care. I charge customers for my time, and that includes the time I spend traveling to their job site. I've paid my dues. Piss on him.

The electrician had originally told me he could save me money by giving me wholesale prices on the light fixtures if

I ordered them from him. However, when all was said and done, I was billed at retail prices. When I argued with him over this, he maintained that I had misunderstood. At this point, it was water under the bridge and another hard lesson learned: get everything in writing, down to the smallest detail. As President Reagan once insisted, with regard to the Soviet Union, "Trust but verify."

One day, late that summer, I was struck with good fortune. I had driven out to Wickes Lumber in Rudyard, just south of the Soo, to look for some interior pine doors, and as I drove up, I noticed a large stack of wooden windows under its sale canopy. They were heavy-duty, double-hung windows with true-divided lights, similar to the pricey Marvin windows I had checked on earlier. They were in excellent shape and had the old-fashioned rope-and-brass weights with pulleys. All of the windows even came with storm windows. I inquired about their origin and discovered they had been removed from the light keeper's house at Whitefish Point during renovations. At eighty dollars apiece, I knew these wouldn't be for sale long. Our sunroom toward the back of the house on the water's side was going to be a screened-in porch, to offer us a cool place to sit on a warm summer day and be a refuge from the tormenting mosquitoes. But when I saw these windows and realized their historical significance, I quickly began to redesign the sunroom layout in my head. Not wanting to return home first and measure and possibly miss them, I purchased eight sets of windows and hauled them home. It was the best piece of luck I'd had in months; I had probably saved over $1000 in window expenses alone. In the sunroom over the next few months, we managed to work five of the light keeper's windows around a plate glass picture window that created a space in which I would someday be spending many happy hours. It would become our favorite room for summer relaxation.

Despite the endless list of jobs, we felt we were making noticeable progress. In designing the log stairway that went from the first floor to the second, we had changed it slightly from a straight stairway to an L-shape so it would add a little more visual interest. We contracted Maple Island to build the log stairway in two separate sections. Then we constructed the platform according to the blueprints while the company built the two stair sections with the appropriate rise and run so we could position them properly. One section would sit on a stair platform and attach to the second floor; the smaller section would sit on the living room floor and attach to the platform. The two sections were delivered in October when Maple Island had brought up the other logs for the walls. The stairs would sit in the middle of the living room for eight months, waiting for us to install them.

If we were to install the log stairway ourselves, we would need four or five strong guys to lift the sections into position. Before lining up the manpower, I measured and re-measured the rise and run. I couldn't believe my eyes. The stairway Maple Island had built was not going to work. The rise was only 7¼ inches instead of the required 7¾ inches. The cumulative error would mean that the top step would have a rise of only about four inches after it was installed, making it a very dangerous feature, especially for anyone walking down those stairs in the night. You naturally expect each stair step to be the same height so you won't stumble. It was an open invitation to an accident someday. We could not accept it.

We immediately called Maple Island to report the mistake, and it agreed to build another set of stairs with the right specs. Six weeks later, the company delivered them to us. There was no shortage of work to do while we waited. This time we measured again very carefully; unbelievably, the company had constructed the correct rise but the wrong run.

If we used these stairs, they would land in the very middle of the platform, way out of position to make the ninety-degree turn. They would have to rebuild them again.

We were beside ourselves. *How,* we wondered, *could a reputable company screw this up twice in a row?* The company was not happy about the news when we reported it to them, but our contract called for a very specific set of stairs. It finally took three attempts to get it right. Since the other two sets of stairs were of no use to anyone else, the company told us to keep them at no charge. We wound up chain-sawing the extra stairs to fit the front and back decks outside. So much for the old carpenter's adage: measure twice, cut once.

In the summer of 1992, my son Travis was five years old. We had sold our house in Traverse City and moved up to the Soo, staying temporarily with my parents. My wife Judy had given birth to our second son, Coleman, in October of '91. That summer, while we were living in town, I purchased my neighbor's fourteen-foot metal rowboat for fifty dollars. I fixed the leaky seams, replaced a couple of wooden seats, and painted it green. We christened it *Turtle*, after Travis' favorite TV series. It would serve as our fishing boat in the bay.

I looked forward to creating a life in which I could take my sons out in the rowboat while they were young and show them the simple joys of perch fishing with a bobber. Over the years, I had never been much of a fisherman, but as a teenager, I had done my share of fishing with my friends. As a kid, I had always hoped my dad would take me out fishing like other kids' fathers in the neighborhood. But my dad was neither a hunter nor a fisherman; he was a soldier in the U.S. Army and worked every day in an office setting. I wanted my sons to experience some of the things I had missed growing up.

One summer morning, Travis and I decided to take *Turtle* out on its maiden voyage for a little perch fishing. This would be his first experience stalking the wily yellow perch. By 7:00 a.m., we had picked up some fresh nightcrawlers and arrived at our half-built log home. When we climbed down the steep embankment to the water, we discovered that our boat, which sat on the shallow sand beach, was filled to the gunnels with sand, water, and reeds. I had not been down there for several weeks and didn't realize how vulnerable our boat might be to the wave action. Not wanting to disappoint Travis by calling the whole thing off, I began bailing like a madman. Travis sat on a nearby log with his new fishing pole and his brown lunch sack, patiently waiting while I reminded him regularly, "It won't be long now." Forty-five minutes later, sweating profusely, I lifted Travis into the boat and we shoved off.

It was a beautiful summer morning; the ore freighters were gliding by farther out in the channel. The hazy morning mist that had settled over the bay was just lifting as we rowed out past the bed of reeds and dropped anchor. For several hours, we cast our lines and couldn't seem to get many bites, but we had a great opportunity to talk with each other and just enjoy the experience of being out there together. Before the morning ended, we managed to hook one whopping six-inch perch and brought it home as proof that we hadn't been skunked.

Day by day, season after season, we kept chipping away at the punch list of jobs that needed to be finished. All of us grew more fatigued and worn out. By the beginning of the third year of building, I was both mentally exhausted and physically drained. We had made a great deal of progress, but it was at a much slower pace than we had expected. At the current pace, I figured it might take as long as ten years to complete this project.

Through carelessness, which is often born of fatigue, I'd had my share of close calls. Any kind of construction—crawling across roofs, climbing on ladders, working with power tools—is hazardous to your health if you are not paying constant attention. One morning, I was working by myself in the second floor bathroom chiseling out the log arch. The flooring had only been nailed down as far as the arch, so as I hopped back and forth chiseling, I lost track of where I was and stepped into the wide open space between the log joists. As I was falling through the floor, I instinctively reached out and grabbed the floor joist with my left hand. That broke my fall slightly, but I wound up with a hairline fracture to my wrist that took four months to heal.

When we had started roofing the house many months earlier, I became so comfortable up there that one day, when I was walking backwards to unroll the roof felt underlayment, I got to the end of the roll. When I looked behind me to see how much more I had to finish, I discovered I was only one step away from walking completely off the roof, an easy twenty-foot drop. That taught me always to stay alert and keep my wits about me when my feet weren't directly on the ground. A trip to the emergency room was just a careless heartbeat away.

Another time, I was standing on an eight-foot stepladder, using an auto-body grinder to bevel some of the exterior log posts. I leaned way out to finish the bevel, and in a split second, I was slammed to the ground, landing on my back. Luckily, I wasn't injured, but again I learned to be more cautious on a ladder.

A building site is a dangerous place for anyone, and sometimes, I felt thankful to be working alone. I realized what a great danger I could be to those around me when unpredictable things happened. One day I was by myself chain-sawing a notch in the upstairs bedroom to fit a partition wall against the log wall. Suddenly, my chain loosened up and shot across the room like a rocket, striking the far wall like exploding shrapnel. No one was hurt, but it was too close a call.

Month by month, we made slow but steady progress. I bought a load of ash flooring from a fellow in Canada and laid our living room floor. I probably should have rented a flooring nailer, but I completed it all by hand. We gave it a light sanding and finished it with a clear water-based topcoat. The kitchen, dining room, hallways, porches, and bathrooms were finished off with ceramic tile flooring. It was very slow and tedious work that required great patience to complete. To this day, I hate cutting cement board, the underlayment for ceramic tile; it is so aggravating to work with. There wasn't a great deal of drywall to install and paint, but much of that was unbelievably slow-going. The drywall had to be scribed and fitted so it could be notched into the logs for a custom fit.

As previously mentioned, Judy helped out considerably with the clearing of the land and the chinking of the logs until she was well along in her pregnancy. My brother Fred was there from the very beginning, helping out on every nasty or grueling job that came along. Without him, we would never have come so far. On the days when the work was starting to get to me physically and mentally, Fred was right there beside me working away without complaint, and usually with a good dose of his dry, understated humor. I had asked him early on to keep track of his hours so I could compensate him. One evening, after about six straight weeks of work, I asked him to write me out a bill. He ignored my request for a while until I insisted that he give me a bill for his services. Finally, Fred handed me a small piece of paper on which he had written what I owed him to date: "One jar of pickled eggs and a case of Guinness Stout." He refused to accept any money. For a moment, I was stunned, but he insisted. I would have to figure out some way to pay him back eventually for all his hard work. We hadn't counted on it, but, in hindsight, we could not have done this without his help. He played an essential role that lightened our burden in ways that could not be measured.

Chapter 7

Old Neighborhoods

Why do you go away? So that you can come back. So that you can see the place you came from with new eyes and extra colors.

— **Terry Pratchett**, *A Hat Full of Sky*

On a steamy August night, I meander on foot through the streets of old Soo neighborhoods where I grew up many years ago. The heavy cool dampness in the night air, a likely sign of an approaching thunderstorm, reminds me of events that took place here long ago, in some of the many houses where my family lived on the south side of town. They were rental houses for the most part, sided with clapboard or asphalt shingles since that was the only affordable way at the time. The rentals had to be within walking distance of schools and downtown grocery stores since my family did not own a car.

Over the years, my family has lived in nearly twenty different houses all across town. Averaging only a year or two in each house, we rented, not just because we couldn't afford a down payment, but also to avoid being tied down. My mother seemed to think that owning one's own home, like most so-called normal families, would practically chain us to a life in the Soo forever. Surely, she believed, the grass and other opportunities would be greener somewhere else. As we were growing up, the ground under our feet always felt shaky and uncertain. Perhaps that is why I wanted someday to build my own home—to plant my family and myself firmly in one spot for a while and never to have to answer the call of a landlord on rent day.

I stroll past a small, pale-yellow one-and-a-half story house at 305 Newton Avenue, where I lived when I was seven and eight years old. It was 1959, and my family had just returned to the Soo after living in Wurzburg, Germany for two years. As I walk past the old house now, neighborhood kids, Melvin and Butch, come to mind. They had discovered innovative ways of getting ahead in the world, the petty thievery of stealing pop bottles from open garages or pilfering chips and peanuts from an unlocked neighbor's Red Dot delivery truck. I quickly learned every trick they could teach me and might have followed a life of juvenile crime until our family pulled up stakes and abruptly moved to a new neighborhood. This is where I first learned to ride a bicycle and where I bashfully received my first kiss from a girl. At this innocent age, I discovered the excitement of climbing to the top of a towering tree, having no fear, and trusting not only the limbs and branches but the rest of the world completely.

The moon is out now, visible through the swaying branches and charcoal clouds. Three blocks away, 1111 Young Street appears . . . a small two-bedroom house on one floor for four boys, one girl, and my mother, who slept on the couch. The landlady would promptly appear at our front door on the first day of every month to collect her rent. My mother would plead for another week's time, saying she didn't have the money. The house was suddenly sold from under us and the sheriff gave our family a final notice, threatening to move our goods out onto the street if we didn't "vacate the premises."

A half-mile's walk westward, just below the hill from

Neville's store, is a plain white, lap-sided frame home: 1110 Tweed Street. A single streetlight, swirling with a frenzy of shad flies, illuminates the front porch. From here, it was a nine-block walk to Lincoln School for me, a one-mile trudge to the high school for my brothers. My faithful black mutt, Daisy, would wait patiently on the front porch steps for the daily appearance of our hostile mailman. In defense of her home turf, Daisy was truly not interested in biting him but only in earning his grudging respect.

When winter approached, we seemed to run out of fuel oil on a regular basis. My mother piled extra coats and blankets on us as we lay shivering in bed until morning, when we were hurried off to school where it was warm. Lincoln School was a fairly happy place where I first learned how to play drums and hook cars. "Hooking" was practically an art in my neighborhood; wearing smooth-soled rubber galoshes, you furtively grabbed hold of a car's rear bumper as it pulled up to a stop sign and hung on for as long as you could down the snow-packed road. In the winter, my fourth grade teacher, Mrs. Ryan, would occasionally reward us for helping to clean the classroom after school by allowing us to grab on to the back bumper of her Rambler as she fishtailed her way home down the snow-covered streets. We usually lasted about four or five blocks before tumbling off on some dry patch of pavement. This was our extracurricular education outside the classroom.

Walking past the old Tweed Street homestead, I see all the kids from the old neighborhood: the Kaplans, the Sepalas, the Bertrams, the Currys and Barcellis, the Baumlers and Walkers. Always something fun was going on—building forts, playing street hockey under the lamplights, chasing squirrels with slingshots through the cemetery, camping out in backyards, raiding gardens . . . the Soo Theater on Saturday afternoons, the old Carnegie Library on rainy summer days. Never a lack of entertainment, and long before the advent of video games, cellphones, and the Internet.

That afternoon in 1963 when President Kennedy was shot in Dallas, I was attending sixth grade at Lincoln School. Upon hearing the stunning news, our teacher solemnly sent us home early, where we watched and listened to Walter Cronkite on a small black-and-white TV as he narrated this national nightmare. Within a year, the country's depressed mood changed abruptly as Beatlemania swept the country, and music was never the same again.

It is near midnight now as I wander through the streets, many of the houses completely dark, some with only a porch light on. Every few blocks I come across some familiar setting that triggers another flash of memory. One of my favorite haunts growing up was 1010 Minneapolis Street, a former apartment house we had rented as a single home. Upstairs, the kitchen and living room became bedrooms; the downstairs living room was converted into a rec room of sorts with a bumper pool table, every guy's teenage fantasy. Friends spent many an evening and weekend with us sharpening their shooting skills. My dad had taught Fred and me how to play bumper pool at the Brunswick Hotel one evening near Christmas. He had just returned on the Greyhound bus for a few weeks leave from the Army in Virginia.

This is the house we lived in twice. When my father was stationed in Fort Sill, Oklahoma, we had moved away for a year, until he shipped out to Vietnam. We returned to the Soo, living temporarily in one room at the Del Mar Hotel, then for a few months at the Rip Van Motel across from the Soo Locks, before returning to the house on Minneapolis.

A thirty-foot spruce tree grew in the front yard, close to the porch. Occasionally, when we came home from school and found ourselves locked out, we would shinny up the tree and crawl in a bedroom window. But most importantly, Minneapolis was where, at the age of fifteen, I met my future wife while she was babysitting and hula-hooping a few doors away. If I hadn't been in that exact place on that particular evening, I might have never met her, and my life would have been completely different.

This is also where my friends and I, in the late '60s, formed our first serious rock 'n' roll band, at a time when great music was taking over the airwaves: the Doors, the Rolling Stones, the Beatles, the Turtles, the Zombies, the Kinks. When I was in the eighth grade, living in Oklahoma, my mom had bought me my first set of Ludwig drums. Practicing them every chance I had, I'm sure I drove some of the neighbors crazy. But those drums paid off in the end. Our band played quite a few sock hops, dances, and mixers, though we never made a dime to speak of after renting out microphones, amps, and PA systems. We always had a blast rehearsing and playing in front of a live crowd, and my interest in music would last a lifetime.

The Minneapolis house is also where my mother, at fifty-five years of age and after two years of night school, finally graduated from high school. She had always regretted dropping out many years earlier and finally felt a great sense of accomplishment in finishing what she had started. A year later, my mother headed off to Switzerland by herself to attend my sister Trisch's wedding. It was one of the highlights of her life.

I meander through the streets a few blocks further south and come across our old 1305 Young Street place where we stayed for about two-and-a-half years. It had a musty old wine cellar in the basement where our Italian landlord once fermented numerous batches of Paisano. I had graduated from high school there, then hitchhiked out to Boston that summer with a friend. It was my first chance to break away from the quiet, small town family life and live independently for a while. The following summer, I narrowly escaped the draft by pulling a high lottery number, then decided to apply for my Merchant Marine card and ship out as a deckhand on the lake freighters. It would help pay for my upcoming college expenses in Ann Arbor. The landlord eventually moved back into his rental and forced us, once again, to find another place to live. It all made me wonder whether, in a former life, my family had been a band of gypsies.

But the gypsy life did have its advantages. As kids, we quickly learned to adapt to new neighborhoods and to make new friends wherever we lived. Growing up in a small town, we never really lost our old friends when we moved; we simply traveled in larger circles, like revolving planets. Moving so frequently, we rarely had the burden of accumulating too much baggage. Family and personal possessions were kept to a minimum, like a snake shedding its old skin on a regular basis. (To this day, I marvel at my brother Bill's ability to travel, at a moment's notice, with only a toothbrush in his pocket.)

For a short time, we lived on 903 John Street, a three-bedroom place, still on the south side of town and only a block from the A&P. When you don't own a car for carrying groceries, location becomes a significant factor. One of my most interesting memories living there was the time my brother Fred, just before leaving on a week-long camping trip to Canada, asked my mother to please remember every day to water the "tomato" plants he was growing in the closet. She was convinced that her ambitious son was a budding farmer. She marveled that he had such a green thumb and loved the great outdoors, no doubt taking after her side of the family. When he returned from his trip a week later and anxiously raced upstairs to check on his closeted-crop, he found the plants dried and frazzled and the dirt as bone-dry and cracked as a desert river gulch. When he asked why she hadn't watered them, my mother replied, "Oh hell, I had chores to do and bills to pay. Sorry, dear; don't worry; they're only tomatoes. I'll buy you some more at the A&P." And, to this day, that may help explain why Fred never successfully pursued marijuana farming, or any other agrarian interest, as a career. Instead, his forte shifted to photography and cooking. After living there for only eight months, we were forced to move again when the place was sold from beneath us.

By leading the gypsy life, we stayed one leap ahead of the law, and yet my family's only crime was that we did not own our own house. Perhaps renting all those years was more practical, avoiding the ambiguities of an uncertain marriage, and refusing to sink roots and make commitments to any one place. If things didn't work out, one could leave at the drop of a hat. It was never the most stable or reassuring situation, but even nomads, sooner or later, learn to adjust.

The granddaddy of all rentals was the move to 313 Amanda. My family managed to last for fourteen years in that house, until 1985—no thanks to a negligent landlord who refused to fix leaky pipes, would not hire an exterminator to clear the nesting squirrels from the attic, and did not want to hear any more particulars about the occasionally flooded basement. Apparently, we were responsible for any repair bills unless we wanted an abrupt increase in the monthly rent.

It was just a matter of time before the water pipes froze one particular sub-zero Christmas Eve and exploded the following morning in a shower of icy water and plaster over the kitchen stove, just as the turkey was about to be slid into the oven. For the next twenty minutes, it was total chaos as family members and company ran back and forth shutting off water pressure in the basement and picking up soggy chunks of plaster and debris from what used to be a normal kitchen. Meanwhile, my mother, who had stayed awake all night drinking coffee and stuffing stockings, was upstairs, innocently wrapping the last of her holiday presents. When calm was finally restored, a six-foot gaping hole overhead, surrounded by dripping lath strips and broken pipes, stared smugly down at us. It was an abrupt and unsettling start to our holiday, but to our company, we just smiled and carried on as if it were a normal Christmas morning. You can never underestimate the potential of a rickety old house when it's twenty-five degrees below zero.

Standing on the sidewalk in front of the Amanda house this sultry summer night, I could see how the front and back porches were sagging heavily and how the exterior had not seen a fresh coat of paint in probably forty years. Without too much effort, my parents could have easily lived out the rest of their days in this place. However, along with my brothers and sister, we decided it would be a good thing for my parents, who were then in their early seventies, finally to own their own place. They had ridden the rental merry-go-round for far too long. So we all chipped in for a down payment on a modest, two-story house at 713 Court Street, directly across from a supermarket. Since my parents didn't own a car, they could walk across the street for their groceries. For the first time in their lives, there was no landlord to collect the rent. Of course, my mother was quick to remind us: "Don't think this old house is going to keep me in the Soo. I'm moving to California one of these days, and don't try to stop me! I'm not living in this iceberg of a town forever!" My father took most matters in stride, but my mother was worn down by the long, bone-chilling winters. Sometimes, hope is enough to get you through the rough spots as you anticipate a better life.

Warm raindrops fall gently on my face; thunder rumbles in the distance, and the wind begins to stir in the trees. As I have been walking these streets tonight, my past has come alive, sparked by memories of the many homes I've lived in. The voices and events of so many years ago will always be accessible to me whenever I please simply by strolling through familiar haunts. How distant memories from old neighborhoods shape our future or guide our choices, one can only guess. But I sense a strong current from the distant past, flowing through me, informing every choice in the present. Perhaps some of these voices from long ago steer us in a certain direction and help us to understand the human beings we someday become and the dreams we pursue. As William Faulkner once wrote, "The past is never dead. It's not even past."[34]

Growing up in the U.P., my family had roots, and yet, in some ways, we had none. We drifted like tumbleweeds through countless neighborhoods, blown with the wind, seemingly vulnerable to the whims of indifferent landlords. My family was always renting and moving from house to house, always making new friends in new neighborhoods. Although we quickly learned to adapt to change, the constant disruption undermined family stability. Now that Judy and I had a growing family of our own, it was time for us to settle down to a more secure and dependable life. The building of our new log home would, hopefully, help us to put down roots that would anchor us for a long, long time. Perhaps living here would allow us to grow old gracefully, happily lost in the woods.

Chapter 8

Briars and Brambles

The gem cannot be polished without friction, nor man perfected without trials.

— **Chinese proverb**

From summer rains to winter snows, year by year, construction on the log home continued, progressing ever so slowly but showing hopeful signs that the end was almost in sight. Meanwhile, as we focused mainly on our log-building agenda, other equally important events began to swirl unpredictably around our lives. As the old saying goes, nothing ever happens in a vacuum; one event impacts many others. It was time to breathe life into some of the plans that had been languishing in the closet for years.

By the summer of 1992, we had sold our house in Traverse City and moved in with my mom and dad in the Soo. My son Coleman had been born eight months earlier, so the four of us moved in and shared one bedroom upstairs in my parents' older two-story Court Street house. After the new baby was born, my wife stayed in Traverse City with the two boys to get Travis started in school and to show our house to prospective buyers. It took over a year to sell the house, so I spent a fair amount of time commuting back and forth. With seven of us sharing the house now, including my brother Fred, it seemed a little cramped and congested, but we hoped this situation would be only temporary. If we worked diligently, our home would be ready soon, or so we hoped. To make things a little easier, we helped out whenever we could with housekeeping, meals, and groceries.

They say that life happens while we're making other plans. Raising a young family, trying to start a new business, and building a house—all of this became quite a juggling act for us. Maintaining our sanity often proved to be a challenge. Sometimes, I felt much more productive when there was a lot on my plate. It required more effective time management, focus, and organization. Without question, time was of the essence. As a result, I became an inveterate list-maker: a punch list of steps to make our new business a reality, a running list of ongoing building tasks, as well as personal notes on school activities for the kids. If nothing else, lists kept me on track and headed in the right direction. Of course, life often has its unforeseen detours, whether we like it or not.

In the early summer of 1991, at the age of seventy-six, my dad had been diagnosed with prostate cancer. Things went rapidly downhill for him, and by late summer, he was bedridden and unable to walk without assistance. Soon, a steady stream of nurses flowed in and out of the house on a daily basis, along with a barrage of medications. Dad seemed to take it all in stride with his dry sense of humor, joking regularly with everyone. It wasn't long before hospice volunteers and home health aides showed up to help out with some of the daily chores. They asked that one of us be present in the house at all times for my dad's sake, but scheduling that block of time was difficult. Fred ran a summer house-painting business, and I needed to work on the new house practically every day. But we managed to work out a time schedule so someone was always nearby.

My dad was the sort of person who would rarely tell anyone if he had a health issue. Like any good Finlander, he just bore it stoically and went on with his life. *Why bother others with your problems?* he may have thought. *They have enough to worry about.* Two years earlier, when I was living in TC, I received a phone call one morning from my sister Trisch in California. With a touch of alarm in her voice, she asked me whether I knew where Dad was at that very moment. It seems he had recently arrived by himself at the Northern Michigan Hospital in Petoskey, about ninety miles south of the Soo. Apparently, he had slipped quietly out of the house, climbed aboard a Greyhound bus to Petoskey, walked several blocks up to the hospital, and said to the receptionist, "Hi. I'm Norm Hill, and I'm here for my triple-heart bypass." The nurse asked whether anyone had accompanied him downstate for the operation, but he had told no one, thinking perhaps that the whole thing would be as cut and dried as a trip to the barbershop. No one at home owned a car, and he didn't really want to burden me by asking for transportation when good old, reliable Greyhound was just around the corner. I quickly rushed up to the Soo, picked up my brother Fred, and raced back to Petoskey. Some would say this was a classic case of Finnish *sisu.* My dad would probably say it was just a matter of "gettin' the old job done."

By late August, we realized that Dad needed more round-the-clock nursing care than we could provide at home. We started to search for nursing homes in the area, but one of the local facilities, upon visiting and talking with the people who ran it, seemed unfriendly and more like a warehouse for the sick and elderly. We passed on that one and finally located a very warm and hospitable place near Marquette in the central U.P., the Jacobetti Veterans Facility. Although we would have to drive three hours in order to visit him, we felt a world of difference in the way the residents were treated there. The entire staff seemed very kind and considerate and took plenty of time to answer all of our many questions. As another plus, my dad's brother Emil and a few other relatives lived nearby and could visit him more regularly.

As I look back, I'm glad that, nine months earlier, on Thanksgiving Day, Dad had come out to look at the early stages of the new house. We hadn't planned it quite this way. Normally, we would have spent Thanksgiving Day at my folks' house watching the traditional Detroit Lions football game on TV and sat down to dinner later that evening. However, the football broadcast went haywire partway through the game. We thought that, while the turkey was roasting in the oven, we might pick up the transmission better out at the new house if we brought a small portable TV and a pair of rabbit ears. We were able to pull in a snowy reception of the game over one of the Canadian stations, but we also had the chance to give Dad a tour of the future house. He was impressed with the scale of the design as well as the massiveness of the pine logs. Before too long, I was hoping to invite him and the rest of our family out for our first Thanksgiving feast in the new place. Sadly, however, that would be the only time Dad ever visited the house. But since Dad was an avid letter writer, we kept him posted on our construction progress with frequent cards and pictures.

For several years, Judy and I had been planning the start of our new business enterprise, Whitefish Bay Furniture Company. As a ready-to-finish furniture store, it would feature custom finishing as well as art, books, and rustic décor. Hopefully, I would be able to design some of my own furniture pieces and work them into the inventory. I would be responsible for accounting and ordering product; Judy would handle the store layout and manage the business. For a long time, we searched Sault Ste. Marie for a desirable building, preferably 3000 to 4000 square feet in an easily accessible, high traffic location. After looking at more than a dozen prospective spots, we found nothing that matched our criteria. Either the rental space was located in some obscure area of town, the rent was ridiculous, or the space was too small or needed serious renovation. For a very long time, we could not seem to find an acceptable location.

Meanwhile, we gathered information about trade shows around the country for unfinished furniture and soon flew to our first major trade show in Atlanta. It was an overwhelming and intoxicating experience to walk the floor of the convention center for days, talking to manufacturers from around the country, and simply smelling the fresh scent of unfinished pine, oak, alder, and maple furniture. Now, for the first time, we could genuinely imagine what a new store in Sault Ste. Marie might look like. We attended most of the seminars on finishing furniture, setting up attractive displays, and working with customers. Everyone we met was more than willing to share his or her experience and expertise with a couple of rookies. We returned home with a briefcase full of furniture company catalogs, fired up with an eager anticipation to start the new business.

By early 1994, we had been working on the log house nonstop for three-and-a-half years. At last, an attractive location at the Soo Plaza showed up in our search, a 3600-square-foot store with plenty of free parking out front for customers. Over several months, we worked out a three-year, renewable, triple-net lease with the landlord and immediately scheduled the many necessary renovations—new partition walls, carpeting, painting, and fixtures. We would need three to four months to renovate the space and order and assemble all our inventory. A long list of things had to be done before opening the store—setting up an office, bank accounts, advertising, ordering product, signage, and most importantly, hiring and training the right employees.

As hectic as those last months were before opening Whitefish Bay Furniture, along with working on the house at the same time, we managed to open officially on May 15, 1994. Originally, my worst-case scenario had been that the house would have been finished in the fall of 1992, and the business would have been up and running by then. What kind of a fantasy life had I been living? Everything was taking two to three times longer than I had estimated. Murphy's Law always seemed to be part of the equation, no matter what our plans, so we always had to factor it in.

We ordered $50,000 worth of inventory and crossed our fingers, hoping for the best. Our Grand Opening was a great success, raising awareness of the new store in the community, but we were still learning the ropes of this business every day. Working forty to fifty hours a week at the store left only evenings and some weekends to work on finishing the house. So, of course, the pace of progress stalled for a while as we focused on the new business. At a time like this, we were so fortunate to have willing grandparents to help out with childcare, not to mention dog care. We were burning the candle at both ends, with no room for error.

Every month, some of my family members took turns visiting Dad up in Marquette. We exchanged letters frequently and updated him on the progress of the log home project. When Coleman was born, we drove over to Jacobetti to introduce him to his grandpa. Dad had originally been given about six months to live, but he was outlasting the doctors' prognosis and had adjusted to his new surroundings quite well. At Christmas in 1992, he was becoming frailer every month, but he wanted to come home for the holiday to spend time with his family. The transition out of the hospital setting and the long three-hour drive over icy roads wasn't the most comfortable, but Dad didn't complain. He enjoyed opening presents and the traditional late-night Christmas dinner, but he was easily tired out and ready to return within a few days. As an Army vet, he had completed his last mission and was ready to retire. In September of 1993, Dad passed away and was buried in Ishpeming, next to his father William, the mining inspector who had been killed in the 1926 Barnes-Hecker mining disaster. Dad was seventy-nine.

By November of 1993, the house was far from being finished, but the bare minimum for living in the house had been completed. We had electric baseboard heating and a wood furnace installed; the water was running in the kitchen and the basement bathroom; the bathtub on the first floor had just been hooked up; and the kitchen cabinets had finally been hung. Two weeks before Thanksgiving, we made the move. My wife and I shared one of the upstairs bedrooms with our two young boys. There were no available beds yet, so we spread our three large mattresses across the pine floor. It was like having ten acres of sleeping area, Japanese style. The kids thought it was great, especially for late-night pillow fights and tumbling. Winter was just around the corner, and at last, we were living on our own as a family.

We had been staying at my parents' house in town for nearly two years, so we figured it was well past time for us to move out, before the cold weather settled in. It was a major change for me to have kids running through the house while I was trying to work on it. My tools were scattered throughout the house, from the basement to the garage. The kids would pick up a few handsaws and a hammer and go off to play somewhere. The following spring, I would find many of my tools out in the nearby woods as the snow melted, covered with a fine coating of rust. The kids must have been building some kind of fort. I soon realized it was necessary to isolate one room at a time so I could work there, make a mess, and leave all my tools in the same place.

With a card table and four stools, we set up our temporary dining arrangements. We decided to hold off buying too much furniture until we had opened our own store and could purchase it wholesale. So cardboard boxes became temporary coffee tables and end tables. We soon picked up a few chairs and table lamps at the Salvation Army store to fill in the gaps temporarily.

The previous summer, a couple of months before moving in, we had purchased a washer and dryer and installed them in the basement utility room. The washing machine was connected to an ejector pump in order to pump the waste water up to the septic tank outside. One morning when I arrived at the house to start work, I walked down to the basement, looking for some tools, and discovered a foot of water on the floor. Had a water pipe burst? Had the basement toilet backed up? I wasn't sure. The last thing I had done the night before was to throw a load of dirty clothes in the washer. After ruling out a bursted pipe, I waded through the water, lifted the top cover off the ejector pump, and felt around, wondering why it hadn't kicked in yet. Sure enough, a lot of debris was clogging up the pump. I went to the garage, got the wet-dry vacuum, and began sucking up all the water off the floor. Finally, I shined a flashlight down into the pump opening for a look. As it turns out, the plumber, when he was notching holes in the studs a few days earlier, had cleaned up his mess by kicking the leftover wood scraps into the hole and putting the cover on. I guess that was easier than using a simple broom and dust pan.

Before long, I discovered I could no longer make a mess and just leave it until the next day. People were living here now, which required a whole different set of rules. Certain rooms were, in theory, off limits until they were completed. After dinner each evening, I tried to work on one room at a time rather than jump from one job to the next. The pace of progress had definitely slipped back into a lower gear, though we were still pleased to be making headway every week.

We plowed through that first winter without too much wear and tear. Our driveway was nearly 125 feet long, so we parked the two cars at the very end and hand-shoveled a path up to the front door. That seemed to work out fine. I have never been interested in personally owning a snow blower for any reason. Not that I'm against them, but according to some of my neighbors, these labor-saving machines tend to break down regularly and have to be hauled into town for repair. After a major snowstorm, I have always been content simply to grab a snow scoop or a good shovel and dig my way out, even if it does take a little longer. I've never understood what all the hurry was about. And it's very good exercise, too, if you don't rush. Besides, with all this aerobic shoveling, there is no need to buy a local gym membership.

U.P. winters usually last about a month longer than the winters in TC. On average, the Soo usually gets about 120 inches of snow every season—sometimes less and sometimes a lot more. By late April, we were safely out of winter's icy grip and ready to plunge into a new business and a new life. Oddly enough, by juggling so many details and responsibilities for so long, we seemed to have gained a newfound confidence in ourselves and learned something about the art of managing chaos.

Chapter 9

Dry Rot

Some men are born mediocre, some men achieve mediocrity, and some men have mediocrity thrust upon them.
— **Joseph Heller**, *Catch-22*

By the time we opened Whitefish Bay Furniture Company in the summer of 1994, we had been working on the log house for four years straight. The new business startup required constant attention—training employees, ordering inventory, delivering furniture, waiting on customers, and so forth. We worked there six days a week, from 9:30 in the morning to 6:00 p.m., and took Sundays off. Learning on the fly, Judy and I were acquiring the skills of managing a business and delegating duties on a daily basis. So many things about operating a new business one can learn only by plunging in and swimming around. And, as we soon discovered, no lifeguards were on duty.

Quite often, semi-truck deliveries arrived at the back door unexpectedly, sometimes just when our finisher had put a fresh coat of varnish on a customer's bookcase or dresser. With the open door, dust and debris quickly settled on the sticky topcoat, prolonging the finishing process. It would be several more years before we had our own warehouse and custom-finishing spray booth. Estimating the cost for a custom finish, at this point, was nothing but a wild guess; we were so new at everything that we hadn't been able to do a time-and-materials study on finishing. We tended to underestimate the labor involved in most jobs. Within a year or two, we had finished enough furniture for customers that we could accurately estimate everything from a roll top desk to a dining room table and chairs. We were finally making a profit on custom finishing.

One of the most difficult tasks to master was putting together special orders for customers. When we were back in the gift industry at Forever Yours in TC, it was a fairly simple matter to special order something for a customer and have it sent by UPS or FedEx. The items were always small and very shippable at the gift store. But now, when someone wanted to custom-order a piece of furniture, we had to build a substantial order to ship cross-country by truck. Most furniture companies have a minimum order of $1000 to $2000, so we couldn't simply order one or two pieces. Freight is also an enormous factor when it comes to furniture. Say, for example, the customer wants to know when to expect his order, but you are still building the truck; you might tell him three to four weeks. But in those next few weeks, if you don't sell enough of that particular manufacturer's pieces, you are not ready to put in an order. Yet you can only sit on customers' orders for so long before they start to get impatient. And you can't blame them; it's not their problem. Over the years, we got ourselves into more hot water over this issue than for any other reason. There was never an easy answer to the dilemma.

As it turns out, working on the endless details of building a house was excellent preparation for running a new business. Both enterprises were started from scratch with no guarantees of success. Learning to plan, coordinate, and execute myriad elements of construction taught us to be thorough and effective in running the business. When unforeseen problems cropped up, we dealt with them head on rather than sweep them under the rug. Contractors didn't always show up when they were expected just as furniture deliveries didn't always arrive when they were scheduled. So we learned to work around these issues and make the necessary adjustments. Occasional frustrations and setbacks would occur in both ventures; we knew to expect that. But if we kept our daily focus on the innumerable details, we trusted that the big picture would take care of itself.

By the time we came home from a day's work and started cooking dinner for the kids, we were running out of steam. The only way for me to get some work done on the house was to say to myself, "OK, tonight I'm going to put one hour into working on the bathroom." Getting started was difficult, but soon, I was over the hump and making headway for the next few hours. In this way, we chipped away at various parts of the house for several months and made slow but steady progress.

All too frequently, we grew very frustrated with subcontractors who did not honor their signed contracts. After the stress-skin panel contractor bailed out on us, the plumber did the same, claiming he was tired of waiting for us so he could finish the next phase of his work. Legally, we could have taken him to court and forced him to complete the job, but we thought about it and decided we would probably get shoddy work from such a disgruntled contractor. It wasn't worth the aggravation.

The electrician and one of the carpenters from TC were overcharging me on their invoices. It was necessary, almost on a regular basis, to comb over each invoice for errors, and then call the guy up to dispute the charges. Other contractors had to be called up each evening in order to line up the expected work for the next several days. Half the time, they never showed up as scheduled, claiming they had to finish up some other job. This tended to become the rule rather than the exception. Was it any wonder that this house was beginning to feel like a deal gone bad, a struggle that might go on endlessly?

Meanwhile, despite the setbacks, I was slowly acquiring many new skills by buying and studying a variety of how-to books on flooring, tiling, and electrical work and approaching each new task as a learning experience. I was soon hanging light fixtures, installing faucets, dry walling, and trimming windows. The work was getting finished, albeit at a very slow pace. But I lay awake in bed many nights worrying over how long it was all taking to finish this overwhelming project—the frustrating issues with subcontractors, the overcharges, the bailouts, the weather, the rising material and labor costs—when would it all end? As I lay there brooding, I could feel dark clouds of self-doubt begin to descend on me. The burden became depressing to the point where I would wake in the morning in a semi-catatonic state, unsure of whether I wanted to do any work that day. I had lost the spring in my step and stumbled into a dead end. *How,* I wondered, *had I dragged myself into such a mess?*

As I walked around town one Sunday afternoon, I glanced admiringly at some of the houses for sale—two-story brick homes near the college, charming Cape Cods on Ashmun hill, rustic cedar homes on the lower river. I daydreamed that I could have simply purchased one of them and saved myself many years of hard work. I was frustrated that I hadn't just hired a general contractor to build us a decent conventional house that would have been completely finished within six months. Why had I gone ahead with this impossible daydream? How could I have been so blind? Surely, somebody should have, could have, warned me of the trouble I was getting myself into. As the old saying goes, "If the hole keeps getting deeper, stop digging." By the time I realized my predicament, I had reached the burnout stage. It was both depressing and mind-numbing. At times, I wished it was just a bad dream that I would wake up from. I thought several times of simply putting it all up for sale and cutting my losses. *Take the financial hit, no matter what it is,* I would tell myself, *and move on to something else. Admit defeat. Would that really be so bad?* I needed a long break, I needed relief, I needed to get away from it all.

The Maple Island Log Home company had neglected to mention so many important things to us: the need to grind down every square inch of the interior logs—surely one of the dirtiest, dustiest, most difficult jobs we had to struggle through; the lack of rebar at critical locations in the log openings for windows and doorways; the inadequate height of the log walls on the second floor, which prevented us from placing the shower where it was supposed to go and also made the installation of second-floor windows on the south side almost impossible. I'm sure that a good many log companies often neglect to mention certain details about working with logs. If they were completely honest with everyone, they'd scare half their customers away. So the customer is left to learn many things the hard way.

Filled with so much anxiety to be finished with this project, I buried my frustration by working harder at the new business. I tried to ignore the tension and the problems that would not go away. Work on the house slowed to a crawl our first year in business. Judy and I wanted to make Whitefish Bay Furniture a successful business, and we were off to a good start. We had confidence in our new business idea, and yet, in the back of our minds, we worried: *What if the business fails and we lose our entire investment? What if our cash flow shrinks and we can't afford the rent any longer? Nobody will bail us out.* It was sink or swim. Fortunately, a steady stream of enthusiastic customers was keeping us quite busy with all the details of operating this new enterprise. By the second year, the business had developed a momentum of its own and didn't seem to require quite as much guidance. It had shifted into third gear and was rolling along much more smoothly.

In the midst of all this bewilderment, I knew I needed a distraction, some kind of diversion to get my mind on other things. A couple of my musician friends asked me to play drums on the weekend at the Cozy Inn in Barbeau, a bar/restaurant about twenty miles from town. It was late November during deer hunting season, and the snow had come early. I had been playing drums off and on in various rock and country bands for twenty-five years, and I jumped at the chance to play again. On weekends, we played music for a rowdy crowd of hunters until one o'clock in the morning, then packed up all the equipment and headed for home. One night, when I was pulling out in my van, a herd of fifteen or so bucks and does dashed right in front of me as I peered wide-eyed through a small patch of frozen windshield. It looked like a stampede. I slammed on the brakes and luckily managed to avoid hitting any of them.

Thankfully, the music had been the best therapy for distraction, reminding me of an activity I loved but had almost forgotten about. Playing drums in the band relaxed me and, for a while, took my mind off my troubles.

Another idea of mine to defuse some of my stress was to get more physical exercise, to work out more aerobically, in order to defuse some of the stress that I was feeling. So I joined a group of young guys in their twenties and thirties who played basketball every noon at the college. I had played pickup hoops over the years and thought I could give it a try. The first ten minutes of the game, I was holding my own, dribbling and passing but not scoring any points. The pace was breakneck, the players racing from end to end with no letup. Suddenly, I found myself sucking wind, gasping for fresh oxygen. I had hit the wall hard and couldn't seem to recover. Should they call the paramedics? How the hell, I wondered, could these guys run like this at such a frantic pace? Obviously, they were in much better physical shape than me; I was definitely out of my league, but I managed to survive the rest of that hour without keeling over. No use in killing myself just for a little fun. I still loved playing basketball, but I would have to work my way up to that level.

Brother Fred

Sometimes, I ask myself why I'm working so hard to help build my brother's house. He'd pay me if I wanted an hourly wage; it's not that. I just like to come and go as I please; I don't want to feel like an indentured servant. This way there's no clock to punch. I'm working on this place because it's a one-of-a-kind opportunity to be part of a very special building process, a custom-built log cabin.

Over the years, I've painted the interiors and exteriors of many houses around town, from one-story bungalows to three-story colonials. But this place calls for some unique skills in roofing, chinking, flooring, and so forth. When it's finished, it's going be one helluva log cabin. We've done more than our share of pure grunt jobs on this house, like having to grind down every square inch of log in the entire building; we were choking on the dust for days afterward, but it had to be done in order to stain and varnish the logs properly. This cabin will probably be in our family for many years to come, so I just wanted to be part of it.

You can't put a monetary value on everything you do. It's nice to have a few bucks once in a while, but I never wanted to be a wage slave. Money has always been overrated. As long as I have enough money to pay my bills, travel cross-country when I like, and afford a good IPA from Founders or Bell's now and then, I'm content. Sometimes, I wish I was flying under the radar and the IRS didn't know I exist; when you're self-employed like me, you pay the IRS dearly for Social Security and Medicare taxes; they nail you hard. I have always been my own boss—no one to answer to, no one to check up on me. I have no wife to tell me how to dress, when to come home, what to eat, how to clean the house, how and where to spend my money. I'm on my own and can do what I please. If I want to watch three NFL games on Sunday, bake a pan of lasagna, and throw down a few beers, who's to say I can't? When you're used to being totally independent for so many years, you're quite comfortable and don't want to change for anybody. For better or worse, that's the life of a bachelor—my house, my rules. You don't hear me complaining though, do you?

In one respect, my brother and I are very similar because we have both been self-employed most of our lives. Neither one of us can stand working for a jerk, taking orders from someone who thinks he knows more than you, if you know what I mean. I worked with my share of assholes when I sailed as a deckhand out on the Great Lakes freighters, the "boats" as they call them. The bosun and mates told me when to eat, when to work, and when to sleep. You barely have a moment to yourself, but when you're at the bottom of the food chain, you have to take what they feed you.

You can never trust a so-called expert, no matter what he tells you. There are so many half-witted bozos in the world who want you to believe this or that. But they don't read much, they don't think for themselves, and they listen to Rush or Fox News to tell them what their opinions should be. Many of them are what my friend Max Klein used to call "book smart, but life dumb." They've been to school for many years but have no practical common sense. So I stay as far away from these jerks as I possibly can. I don't suffer fools easily and want no part of them.

Over the years, whenever I've needed an interesting physical and mental challenge, I've headed off to walk the Appalachian Trail. It runs over 2000 miles from Springer Mountain, Georgia to Mt. Katahdin, Maine. I've hiked various sections of the trail including a 400-mile stretch up and down the thickly forested hills of Georgia with a 115-pound pack on my back. If that doesn't test your physical limits and mental discipline, nothing can. The Appalachian Trail is one of the loneliest but most beautiful places in the world. As it turns out, hiking the trail and carrying a heavy backpack for weeks on end prepared me, in many ways, for the challenge of working on this log home, summer and winter, for months on end. It's up one hill and down the other. At times, you have to reach down inside yourself for those extra reserves. It's too easy to get pissed off at different things when they don't go your way, but there's never a thought of giving up. Never.

We had hired Tom and Tony (TNT Construction) to install the fascia boards and some of the exterior trim. One particular scorching summer day, Hector—one of their coworkers—was about to climb the ladder to apply a piece of trim when he caught sight of a hornet's nest the size of a cantaloupe, right in the spot where he was going to work. Hornets don't usually bother anyone unless you get too close to their nest; then they sound the alarm, attack in numbers, and sting repeatedly. The top of a thirty-foot ladder is no place to be stranded when you are being stung by angry hornets. At that height, there is no safe refuge.

Hector understood this very clearly and insisted there was no way he was working anywhere near a nest that size. Tony stepped up and said he would take care of those hornets, but first he needed a heavy jacket, a roll of duct tape, and a large coffee can. We located a heavy Carhartt work jacket and pants and a thick winter chook. Though it was over eighty degrees outside, Tom and Hector helped Tony into his protective thermal outfit. They were taking no chances: they duct-taped his work gloves to his coat at both wrists and taped his pant legs to his boots at the ankles. He wore a pair of clear goggles over his eyes and wrapped the rest of his face in scarves. He looked like Neil Armstrong about to set foot on the moon. There was no way possible for an angry swarm of hornets to penetrate that kind of armor.

We had thought about using a can of hornet spray that shot twenty feet from the can, but in the middle of the day, that could be dangerous because many of the hornets were coming and going frequently from the nest. It would be more practical to spray a nest just before dark when the hornets were all back inside resting.

With the coffee can in hand, Tony climbed the ladder slowly. We all backed up to the perimeter of the property just in case there was trouble. With one quick motion, Tony slipped the can over the nest, scraped it off the underside of the roof, and slid the plastic lid over it. When he came down the ladder, he duct-taped the lid to the can, reinforcing every possible escape route. Standing twenty feet away, we could hear the angry buzz of the trapped hornets. Hector inched his way closer, not taking his eyes off the can. He wanted to put his ear next to the can to hear the agitated buzz. Tony shook the can like he was making a martini, then put his ear to the side of the can.

"Holy crap! Are they ever pissed in there!" Tony said.

"Let me hear it! Let me hear it!" Hector insisted, nervously approaching the coffee can.

Tony held the can to Hector's ear. His eyes bugged out, his jaw dropped in amazement. The hornets in that can were so riled up, Hector knew, that they wanted to kill somebody, anybody. Right at that moment, Tom crept up behind Hector and goosed him in the nuts. I have never in my life seen anyone leap as high as Hector leaped or scream as loudly as Hector screamed. It was as if he had been shocked by an electric cattle prod. Having jumped completely out of his skin, it took him ten minutes to calm down and catch his breath. Miraculously, no one got bitten and we had a good laugh, but Hector vowed his revenge. To prevent getting badly stung, we carefully disposed of the can of angry hornets. Having been mercilessly attacked by hornets in the past for no apparent reason, I had no qualms about removing them.

We needed these diversions to lighten some of our burden. Thank God for levity; it can be the soul of life whenever things get too serious. I had always believed in finishing what I started, but why, I wondered, was I knocking myself out like this? Thoreau came to mind with his criticism of his neighbors who worked such long, arduous hours running their farms: "Why should we be in such desperate haste to succeed, and in such desperate enterprises?"[35] There is a much simpler way to live one's life, he believed, starting with the reduction of our own material needs. "A man is rich in proportion to the number of things he can afford to let alone."[36] In other words, anyone can learn to be happy with less if he spends his time pursuing activities that are personally meaningful. In hindsight, with four years of labor behind us, I didn't need much convincing that building a simpler wood-framed house would have made great practical sense and saved us from so much needless wear and tear.

For certain, we had bitten off more than we could chew and had a hell of a time admitting it to ourselves. Like a fighter getting whipped in the ring, you can get up off the mat only so many times before realizing you've met your match. Our sense of overall burnout was palpable. Week by week, we came closer to throwing in the towel and accepting the consequences. It wasn't just the sheer size of the constant workload that was so discouraging, but more obviously, this project had stretched out for years longer than we had ever imagined. And now, running a business full-time and raising a family, we would have to shift the home-building project to an even slower pace than before. Money would soon be running out as the payments from the sale of our business in TC came to an end. If our new business was successful, it would carry us toward completion of the house, but not for some time. If it failed, all bets were off.

Judy

Sometimes, it seems like this building project will go on forever. I never dreamed it would take so long to finish this place, and I've been working right along with those guys whenever I can. It wasn't so easy while I was pregnant with my second one, but after that, I helped plenty with the chinking. We had to get all the staining and varnishing of the inside logs finished first. Then came the foam backer rod that had to be stapled in place so the chinking had something to stick to. Applying the chinking was my specialty. Anyone can slap it on and spread it out, but to do a really good job, you have to take your sweet time. Chink is very gooey and sticky and doesn't want to spread very easily unless you squirt it with a little water and tool it with your putty knife. We made a variety of chinking tools to use on the different widths and angles. The best putty knives for chinking are the cheap, real flexible ones; it's way easier to spread a smoother line. For the corners, we used a bent teaspoon.

Now, I hate to brag, but my chink lines are the best in the whole house. It may take me twice as long to do them, but mine are far better. Those guys hate me saying that, but it's true. They say if I had to earn a living chinking by the hour, I would starve. I think they're just jealous. You have to spray on just enough water to get a smooth line; it still runs down all over the logs. You need a lot of paper towels to wipe the edges of your lines, and as I said, I'm very fussy about how they look.

At other times, I run errands for Rich and Fred to the hardware store, picking up screws, nails, and other odds and ends. Now and then, I bring them hot coffee and sandwiches or sometimes a couple of cold ones to give them energy. With all the chain-sawing and grinding and dry-walling, these guys keep making quite a mess, so I come in and try to sweep things up to keep the place looking halfway clean. Like I said, progress on this house is moving along like a glacier, but looking a little better every week. Still, it's taking forever. At this rate, I may be old and gray by the time we move in, but I'm keeping my fingers crossed.

One hundred years from now, when all is said and done, who knows if this log home, started in 1990, will still be standing. If anything manmade is neglected and uncared for, time will inevitably diminish it. Wood, in particular, is especially vulnerable to decay. We learned another lesson the hard way the time we installed two sets of leftover log stairs on the outside deck. The two massive log stairways that had been incorrectly constructed many months earlier were cut down to size with a chain saw. I set them both in place, bolted them to the deck and back porch, and double-coated them with exterior varnish. For several years, they sparkled with a golden glow and were very serviceable. Then gradually, without my knowledge, the feet of both stairways began to rot from the water they had absorbed. In my haste, I had neglected to put any kind of drainage rock or gravel beneath the feet. It was just a short matter of time before they would decay to the point where they could not be repaired. We ripped them out, replaced them with treated lumber, and set them correctly on a bed of pea stone for drainage.

In *A Place of My Own,* Michael Pollan speaks of rot and decay: "The culprit, the chief means by which the forest reclaims any human construction, is the same: water. Lumber may not be alive exactly, but it is still part of the nutrient cycle of the forest and will return to it sooner or later."[37] By protecting the log structure with roofing materials, several coats of finish, and carefully applied chinking, we may have postponed the eventual fate for some years. Time will one day catch up with it. "Like everything else once alive, lumber is on loan from the land and in thrall to water, which, in concert with the conspiracy of insects and microorganisms we call rot, eventually will reduce it to compost."[38] After all our hard work, that's quite an unsettling thought.

Accepting this kind of stark reality doesn't offer me much consolation or reassurance. It makes me wonder why we labor so hard at building some things and attach so much value to certain possessions when, one day, they will simply be dust in the wind. Could we not spend our time in more worthwhile endeavors? How carefully do we consider the repercussions of committing to a specific project before spending years of blood and treasure? Perhaps Thoreau was right after all: simplicity can be its own reward.

Chapter 10

Hair of the Dog

If you're going through hell, keep on going.
— **Winston Churchill**

Years ago, back in high school, I ran cross country for the Sault High Blue Devils. It was a two-mile race, through conditions that ranged from warm sunshine to blowing snow, from high winds to drenching downpours. Sometimes, we raced through the woods, occasionally over a golf course, or around a football field. The pace at the beginning was always faster than I wanted. We were all a bit nervous and felt the adrenaline pumping through our veins, so we took off like a pack of jack rabbits. After two or three minutes, we settled into our stride and relaxed a little, always trying to pass the next guy ahead of us. When I hit my second wind, I seemed to gallop with less effort and breathed more deeply. My body had adjusted to the strain and was now maximizing every muscle, every breath. It was now a mental as well as a physical race. Fighting oxygen depletion and muscle exhaustion, I soon found myself in a struggle of mind over body.

Though I eventually reached my stride while working on the house for several years, it didn't happen all at once. It was more of a slow metamorphosis. Over a long period of time, my attitude toward work gradually evolved to the point where

I learned to focus more on the present, the daily activity I was involved in, rather than the endless punch list of jobs. I decided to stick with one room at a time and finish everything I could before moving to another job in the house. Week by week, I started to notice tangible progress in each section of the house. By looking back at what we had completed so far, rather than how far we had to go, I felt a much greater sense of accomplishment. I wasn't really working any faster than before; it was simply my perception that had changed. I was no longer fighting myself.

Now my mantra was "one day at a time; enjoy the process." I began to pace myself differently. My wife and I took more time off to do a few leisurely things like going out for dinner and attending local basketball and football games. We began taking the kids out more often for ice cream or pizza. For a number of years, the total focus had been strictly on work, work, work—trying to speed up the process of building that was dragging on so long. Our goal had morphed into an overwhelming obsession that was distorting our priorities. Gradually, we found a balance in our lives that had been missing. After we moved into our half-finished house, we adapted to the status quo and just accepted it for what it was. No more racing around frantically to complete a particular job; instead, we simply worked on it in increments at a reasonable pace. The stress of everyday worry was simply not worth the price. The job would be finished when it was finished. If it took a bit longer, so what?

I hadn't given up my *sisu*, my Finnish stubbornness; I was still just as determined to finish this house, but I was able to channel this energy in a calmer, more relaxed way. After work at the store, I came home each night, ate dinner, and put in a couple of hours at such tasks as installing a sink and toilet or building a shower in the first floor bathroom. Before too long, we had applied the ceramic tile in the shower and installed the base cabinets. If I were able to manage a little progress every day, I was content. We trimmed out over sixteen windows, hung fifteen doors, and varnished them. Month by month, we made slow progress—building closets and a pantry, laying a hardwood floor in the living room, and hanging light fixtures throughout the house.

In the master bedroom upstairs sat a 1935 cast iron, claw-foot bathtub that we had confiscated from my parents' house when they renovated their bathroom. It had been reglazed and painstakingly wrestled up to our second floor to await installation. I'm not proud to admit that the bathtub sat there in the bedroom for over a dozen years while I finished various other jobs on the list. At one point, I had suggested planting petunias in it, but my wife didn't seem too interested.

Many of the tools and extra building materials were moved out to the garage, which we had built during the following summer. Ideally, the garage, being a separate building, should have been built first so we would have a staging area for the whole project. Measuring twenty-six feet by thirty-two feet, this garage was intended to be a woodworking shop, a place to design and build furniture. Parking our cars in it was an idle afterthought and very unlikely. TNT had helped us frame and sheath it; then Judy and I took over to save money on its completion. We ordered rough cedar boards from a local sawmill and made our own lap siding on the table saw.

When it came time for roofing, Judy was game enough to climb the ladder to the garage rooftop, and together, we nailed the shingles on. The only real problem came along at the end of the day when we were about to climb down the ladder. As I held a very sturdy industrial ladder up to the garage gable, Judy froze up and could not seem to turn around and step backwards onto it. All afternoon, she had been scampering from one side of the roof to the other like a mountain goat with no sign of fear. But staring at that ladder, she could not bring herself to extend her leg for a foothold. Panic was setting in; the evening light was growing dimmer. The garage gable was the safest spot to mount the ladder, so after a long while, I told her that short of calling for a helicopter rescue, she would have to inch her way onto the ladder and come down. I stood on the upper rungs to guide her while she reluctantly placed her foot on the ladder, shaking nervously, and managed to get to the ground safely. In hindsight, I doubt I would ever make a very reliable fireman. If I ever had to rescue someone from a burning building, throw her over my shoulder, and carry her securely down a long ladder, I think it would be easier just to call for the safety net and say, "Whenever you're ready, jump!"

After a couple of heating seasons, the logs had lost a fair amount of moisture and had settled a great deal. The three-inch gaps we had allowed at the top of each partition stud wall had closed up considerably, so we applied the final pine wall and window trim. Most of the chinking had stayed intact and required only minimal touch-up. Because we had allowed more settling space above all the windows and doors than was suggested, it was not necessary to remove any of them for readjustment. That precaution alone saved us a great deal of time as well as potential grief.

After the main stress-skin paneled roof had been installed, we wound up with a surplus of two good-sized, triangular panels, each measuring about twelve feet by ten feet. They were too good to waste, so we donated them to one of the local bars, where they were joined together to form a sturdy bandstand for the musicians. I guess that's what they call bringing down the house.

As time went on, our new business, Whitefish Bay Furniture, developed a momentum of its own and became much less difficult to operate. We made plenty of mistakes our first couple of years, but we learned what we could from them. Our customer base grew slowly, much of it from word of mouth, and seemed to support our fledgling business. We regularly sent handwritten thank you notes to our customers, and every once in a while, a customer sent us a note back thanking us for the thank you note. A small thing, but they hadn't expected it.

On weekends and as time allowed, we worked on unfinished projects back at the house. By springtime, we were busy spreading topsoil and planting grass seed. Interior cedar log railings in the loft and along the stairway were custom built and finished off. Bookcases and drywall were painted and trimmed out. What was missing now was the tense attitude toward the work, the frantic mindset. In place was a slower, more deliberate rhythm and pace that actually made it more enjoyable as we completed each task. Sure, we still had a long ways to go before completion, but now it became more of a journey and less of a goal. We were thankful to be living in the house now without a mortgage hanging over our heads. By structuring the sale of our business in TC, we had managed to juggle our expenses on a month-to-month basis and to avoid dealing with a bank. After reshuffling the deck, sweat equity had become our ace in the hole.

Tom

Tony and I have been working together on construction jobs for quite some time now. My brother-in-law, Rich, hired us for a variety of carpentry projects on his new cabin; only it's not what I would call a cabin; it's more like a place you'd build for your retirement years: big logs, half-round windows, huge field stone fireplace. Should be a nice place when it's finished.

Rich wanted us to help shingle the roof right in the middle of deer season—Right, like that was going to happen. In the U.P., deer season, which runs from the 15th through the 30th of November, is a sacred time of year. Every hunter I know takes two weeks off to hunt deer, drink beer, play cards, get away from the old lady, and tell a few stories at hunting camp. Rich isn't a deer hunter, so he probably doesn't quite get it. You don't want anything to interfere with deer camp, unless it's an emergency. Anyway, we finished shingling that roof just before Christmas. The weather was nasty, but we finally got it done. Believe me: December is not a good time to be crawling around on a slippery roof.

Besides trimming the gables and eaves with twelve-inch wide fascia boards, we also built a good-sized deck off the side of the house. The following summer, Tony and I helped build the two-car garage; it's not going to be used for parking their cars in; I heard Rich say it's going to be a woodshop for building furniture.

Tony and I work pretty well together most of the time. Sometimes, I'm the boss; sometimes, he's the boss, depending on what mood we're in. I'm very resourceful when it comes to solving problems. And that's mostly what good carpentry is: a problem-solving business. I can always come up with a solution if I think about it long enough. Always been that way ever since I was a kid. I don't have a builder's license and never did. Don't really need one. The license doesn't make you a better builder. Hell, I know guys around town with licenses who I wouldn't trust to build an outhouse, let alone someone's home. Like they say—all hat and no cattle.

During a typical year, I work at more than just carpentry jobs. I do plumbing, dry-walling, some electrical work, and painting. To survive year-round in the U.P., you have to be a jack of all trades. Things slow down for us in the wintertime, but we pick up a few smaller jobs here and there. That leaves me a little more time to get up to the casino to play the slots. I've had more than a few good payoffs on some nights, even though I've probably dropped more dough than I care to admit. But the casino took care of me, in a way, by putting me on its VIP list, which means I get complimentary hotel rooms and meals from time to time. A little gambling helps the winter go by that much faster. Just wish I could hit the Progressive sometime; I hear it's paying over 125 grand. That would sure buy me a lot of new tools and maybe a new pickup. I think my clutch is going out.

One October day, about a month before our family moved in, I was standing on a stepladder in the entryway, varnishing the overhead logs. My blue jeans and sweatshirt were spattered with a mixture of gray chinking, paint, and varnish. My baseball cap and hair reeked of moldy sawdust and sweat. I was working by myself when the front door suddenly opened and in walked a stranger. I said hello to him. He glanced up at me for a second, said nothing, and meandered into the living room. I continued to brush on the varnish as this fellow strolled into the kitchen, checked out the dining room, then trotted upstairs for a look around. Then, as he was about to leave, he said to me, "Nice place here. Whose is it?" "It's mine," I said. "Oh! Oh! I'm sorry," he said, hustling out the door, "I thought you were just one of the workers." I'd never experienced a case of breaking and entering quite like that before.

As local residents are well aware, winters in the U.P. can be brutal. The heavy snow can come early in the season and the wicked cold not far behind. Entering our second winter in the new and still unfinished house, right after Christmas, we experienced a sudden cold spell descending on the Soo area with temperatures of twenty-seven degrees below zero. The chill refused to lift for several days straight.

We had left the old black Dodge Caravan, my work vehicle, parked at the end of our hundred-foot driveway; we managed our holiday visits to relatives in and out of town with my wife's Honda. By the second day of the cold spell, I tried to start up the van, but it just sputtered and whined when I turned the key. We tried jumping the battery from our other car, but to no avail. The engine refused to turn over. Thinking that the gas line or the oil in the pan might be frozen, I rigged up a hundred-watt lightbulb on a trouble light and placed it under the engine, surrounding it with a blanket to hold the heat. Four hours later, I came out in the cold and cranked the engine. No luck, just a mournful gasp and a shudder.

At the business the next day, I happened to be talking with a customer about the bone-chilling temperatures and my stalled-out van. He recommended a strategy I had never contemplated.

"This may sound a little strange to you," he said, "but trust me. This will work! We did this to our old jalopies back in the '30s when they froze up. OK, first you get yourself a pipe or a heavy stick two or three foot long, and you wrap an old rag around it. Then you pour a little kerosene or gasoline over the rag, not too much, and you light it and stick it right under the engine. That'll get her started for sure."

I was in a bit of shock. I didn't want to blow my vehicle to kingdom come; I just wanted the engine to turn over. But my customer insisted his method was foolproof. As he went out the door, I wondered to myself whether he operated a salvage yard in his spare time. I might be bringing him some business.

As it turned out, I had cranked the engine so many times trying to start it that I had warped the engine head. My van was toast until I could find a used replacement engine. We had almost given up on the van when, six months later, our mechanic found another engine, for a reasonable price, that would fit and installed it. My wife began using the newly revived van to drive the kids to school and daycare. She liked it because it was roomy and good on gas.

In early December of 1995, as my wife was dropping my son Travis off at his elementary school, another car suddenly came around the corner of the parking lot and totaled the van. No one was hurt, but the van had to be towed into town and deposited in my brother's driveway. The very next morning, a record-breaking snowstorm whirled into the Soo area and buried the entire city. For four days straight, from December 8 to 11, the snow kept falling and drifting into enormous banks. Virtually every business in town was closed; all the local schools were shut down for a week. The entire area was paralyzed. On the third day, the four of us piled into the pickup truck to try to get to Whitefish Bay Furniture, but we were turned back when the road narrowed to a single lane. Apparently, the weather was worse the closer we got to town. The county plows had been unable to make much headway due to the heavy snows and drifting and could manage to keep only one lane of the highway open.

A number of winter records had been shattered. According to local meteorologist Karl Bohnak:

> The most impressive was the largest storm snowfall in the history of Sault Ste. Marie: 61.7 inches . . . December 1995 became the snowiest month in the history of the Sault with a whopping 98.8 inches; 82.5

> of which came down through the first twelve days of the month. This incredibly snowy month contributed to the all-time season total of 222 inches.[39]

The Michigan National Guard was ordered in to help clear the roads and haul away the massive snow piles. By week's end, not one spare snow shovel, snow scoop, or snow thrower could be found in any hardware store in town. In Soo, Canada, just across the St. Mary's River, one of the malls was closed down due to a partial roof collapse. In the strip mall where our business was located, over five feet of snow rested overhead on our roof. The only help the landlord was able to round up was a couple of college-age boys to shovel by hand. Virtually every last bit of manpower was spoken for. We just prayed that our flat roof didn't collapse from the burden. Mother Nature's devastating power was frightening to behold, and we were at her mercy. She had brought human activity to a standstill, as if to remind us of her fickle ways and awesome strength.

Two months passed. Beneath an enormous white marshmallow in my brother's driveway sat our wrecked Dodge Caravan. After many hours of shoveling and sweating, we were able to free it from its snowy cocoon. The local Ford dealer had told me he could offer me something on a trade-in if I could get the car down to him for an inspection. At first, the engine coughed and spit a few times, ran for a couple of minutes, then cut out. I finally got it running and brushed it off completely, but it looked like hell from the accident. The sheet metal on the front end was bent and crumpled, the paint badly scraped off in many places. Nevertheless, I drove it fearlessly down Ashmun Street, the main thoroughfare in town, across the canal bridge and tried to make a left turn. Although I had rotated the steering wheel as much as possible, the car would not respond. I was blocking traffic, and other drivers began beeping at me to move out of the way. Finally, I hopped out of the van to have a look at the problem. Apparently, the sheet metal near the left front wheel was pushed in enough to prevent the wheel from pivoting. I grabbed hold of the fender with both of my gloved hands and yanked. It was just enough clearance for the tire to make the complete turn, and I was soon on my merry way.

It was a little embarrassing to pull up in front of the Ford showroom with this vibrating heap of crumpled sheet metal, but the salesman came out with his pen and clipboard, a slight smirk on his face, and calmly proceeded to go down his checklist. When all was said and done, he offered me $500 on a trade-in, which I all but jumped at. Between transmission problems, replacing multiple starters, and finding a new engine, the van had been nothing but trouble for me. I was happy to escape from the black hole.

Not all winters in the U.P. are as bad as this particular one. Nevertheless, most residents spend a good part of their time shoveling roofs and sidewalks and snow-blowing their driveways. Outside work slows to a crawl as frozen fingers, toes, and noses become part of the mix. On many a typical winter day, getting from point A to point B can become a real challenge for drivers. You learn to approach icy intersections with great caution due to the polished surface from so many drivers braking and accelerating. Most drivers carry a pair of jumper cables, a good windshield scraper, and a shovel just in case of trouble. Winter blizzards are just a fact of life in the U.P.; you take them in stride and give thanks that it's not something serious like a tornado or hurricane.

Once every year, at a different city around the country, Judy and I attended a national trade show for unfinished furniture. For three days, we shopped for new furniture for the store, attended educational seminars, and caught up with old friends we hadn't seen since the year before. One summer, in 1997, we had flown into Nashville for the show. Having walked all day for several miles up and down the show aisles, talking to manufacturers and friends, we retired back to our hotel for a rest before dinner.

I went into the bathroom to shower and, a few minutes later, came out looking as white as a ghost. Not wanting to frighten my wife, I was uncertain what I should tell her. I had just discharged a large amount of blood in the toilet bowl, even though I felt perfectly fine. Something was definitely not right with me. It was a very sobering moment, but I tried to stay calm and not panic. I was sure there must be a good explanation that, in my state of alarm, I had probably overlooked. But my mind was racing, my imagination fearing the worst.

We got through the last couple of days of the trade show and flew back home. After I arrived at the doctor's office to have it checked, I was sent over to a specialist who did a biopsy. I hoped that perhaps it was a hemorrhoid that had burst or a bleeding ulcer. When the phone rang the next day, the doctor was calling to confirm that I had stage-three colorectal cancer.

Seldom do we get such a cold slap in the face so completely out of the blue. I had not seen it coming at all, had always felt healthy and energetic. Soon, I couldn't help but speculate over the stress of building the house and starting the new business in the past seven years. Had I somehow internalized that long period of tension and done this to myself? Had my diet been way out of line and finally caught up with me? But the more closely I thought about it, the more warning signs I realized I had blindly ignored. Over the past six months, there had been noticeable spots of blood now and then. Nothing persistent. No pain of any kind. Surely, I thought at the time, I could ride out whatever it was—no need to pay attention unless it got worse. I know only too well now how that frame of mind is typically the male viewpoint. Sometimes, I think women outlive men for one reason: they never hesitate about going to the doctor promptly to check out something suspicious. Men tend to procrastinate and, regrettably, wait for more urgent signs of trouble.

Over the next few weeks, my family grew very close to me. We cried many nights, fearing what the future might soon bring. I wished for things I might never see, things I had taken for granted. Would I live long enough to see my sons play high school basketball and graduate? Whom would they marry? What would my grandchildren look like? How would my sons turn out? What would my wife do without me? Would she remarry? On and on, questions like these obsessed me for days until I had exhausted myself. Then, what now felt like more trivial questions had to be considered: Who would finish building this log house we had started? Would it ever be done before my time was up? Who would run the business? How would it survive? The questions were overwhelming, the answers unknowable.

Stage-three cancer was certainly dangerous, but it was not an outright death sentence. My chances were dependent on a number of things. In surgery, the doctor always tries to remove a so-called safe margin around a tumor. Depending on whether or not some of the cancerous cells migrated to other areas, I wouldn't know right away what my long-term prognosis would be. Dr. McCullough, who would operate on me, advised me to go through six weeks of radiation following the surgery as well as several months of chemotherapy. That would kill cancerous cells around the body as well as many healthy ones, and there might be some long-term physical effects from the radiation. The other option was a colostomy, a surgical procedure that serves as a sort of shortcut for the digestive system. It would require the regular use of a plastic pouch to discard waste. However, weighing all the risks, I felt the safest course was to follow Dr. McCullough's advice and take the first option.

After the initial shock of confronting cancer wore off, I felt powerless to change anything. My only way of controlling any events, including my overly active imagination, was to arm myself with as much information about colorectal cancer as possible. At the time, we did not own a computer, so I called the American Cancer Society and asked for all the pertinent written material it could send me so I could thoroughly understand my condition and all of my options. For weeks, I devoured every pamphlet and piece of information that was given to me. Friends offered me books on building up my immunity and strengthening my diet. It was an education by necessity, and I took it seriously. If this was to be a battle, I wanted to fight fully armed.

Finally, after several weeks of frantic speculation, I began to feel much stronger mentally, knowing my particular situation and what my individual choices were. A feeling of calm resolve came over me, and I decided that, come what may, I was going to ride things out with dignity. I had done all I possibly could. There was no room for regrets.

After the ordeal of surgery, radiation, and a week in the hospital from infections, my normal life resumed, at least on the surface. For several more months, I continued the chemotherapy. Before long, I was able to return to full-time work at the business, thankful that the worst part of the whole process was behind me. I would never again be so busy that I couldn't make time for my family; they were now my priority. Without question, this ordeal became a blessing in disguise. Whether it was a problem at the business or an issue about finishing the house, nothing ever seemed to take on the same urgency as before. Worry played a less demanding role and soon became an insignificant matter on my priority list.

Sometimes, it's a good thing to confront one's own mortality; it makes us more human and, hopefully, a little wiser. It gives us a better perspective on life; as Stanford psychologist Laura Carstensen explains: "How we seek to spend our time may depend on how much time we perceive ourselves to have."[40] When we get a clearer sense of our own mortality, our perspective shifts. Although most of us would prefer not to talk or even think about it, our contemplation of death, ironically, brings life into sharper focus. Our priorities realign themselves very quickly.

Former mountains soon became trivial molehills. Issues that had once seemed so important, home-building or business-related, were now greatly diminished, hardly worth getting excited over. In the greater scheme of things, I still took them seriously, but from a more philosophical perspective. In many ways, I felt liberated. Obviously, I wasn't completely out of the woods yet; tomorrow would be another day to deal with. But I had run the gauntlet, for now, and was still standing. What more could I ask?

Chapter 11

What Goes Around . . .

My life has no purpose, no direction, no aim, no meaning, and yet I'm happy. I can't figure it out. What am I doing right?
— **Charles M. Schulz,** *Peanuts* cartoonist

As I write these words, we are now twenty-five summers into this adventure. So much has changed over the years, but now, at least, we have the benefit of hindsight. Has the house finally been completed? Well, no. But it's getting close. Those nagging little unfinished details seem to linger in obscurity. We hardly notice certain things anymore—like an unpainted door frame or missing outlet covers that need to be chiseled to fit into logs—unless we consciously pay attention to them. Surely, we've accepted a certain number of loose ends that will eventually get tied up, but for now that will have to do.

Our experience was a total immersion in the building process, both physically and mentally. We naively underestimated the complexity and overall time frame for a project like this. But once we committed to it, there was no turning back, or so we told ourselves. At many points, I hated to admit to myself, or to anyone for that matter, that we were in way over our heads. Looking back now, it's possible the entire project could have gone either way. Quite often, we felt so overwhelmed by the stress and frustration that we were ready to call it quits and walk away from it all.

Richard Stengel, of *Time* magazine, in an article on Nelson Mandela, had an insightful way of looking at a situation like this: "Life is never either/or. Decisions are complex, and there are always competing factors. To look for simple explanations is the bias of the human brain, but it doesn't correspond to reality. Nothing is ever as straight forward as it appears."[41] Complexity is always easier to deal with when it's broken down into manageable parts. And even then, sometimes, the juggling of the various parts can turn to chaos. Part of the problem was the relentless pace at which we drove ourselves as well as the mile-long, never-ending list of details that always begged to be addressed. We didn't allow ourselves enough time to exhale, to work hard, and then relax. The clock, internally driven, always ticked loudly in our ears, compelling us to finish.

The conditions of work had been self-imposed; no one was actually breathing down our necks. Instead, the deadlines came about from necessity: the need to start a new business soon, the desire to move our family into a completed living space, the looming reality of running out of money. Within several years, partly due to burnout, we changed our entire approach to building. Determined as we were not to give up, taking one day at a time, we began working at a slower, more deliberate pace so we could enjoy the process. We chose a less hurried tempo, a more human rhythm. Each day, with its assorted problems and challenges, would reveal itself, and we would confront those issues one by one and do our best to resolve them. We would no longer sweat the details. What we discovered was that with the right combination of perspective and attitude, we could accomplish things we never thought possible.

By doing so much of the work ourselves, we had saved a bundle of money. But time was swiftly moving on. We began weighing the financial and emotional consequences of hiring out versus completing every job ourselves. The trade-offs were worth considering. Another adjustment was simply learning to live happily in a half-built house. Construction would be going on in adjacent rooms for years to come, but we adapted and made progress the best we could.

One major benefit over the years of construction was the acquisition of so many new skills: from tiling, carpentry, and plumbing to electrical, dry-walling, and landscaping. These skills came in very handy down the road, saving me both time and money by repairing things myself rather than always having to call in a licensed professional.

One by one, we knocked off our long punch list of tasks. That cast iron bathtub that sat in our master bedroom for so many years was eventually installed in the master bathroom and hooked up to brass faucets and brass drainpipes—a real showpiece. Ironically, after such great effort and expense, it rarely gets used; no one bathes anymore—everyone prefers to shower. Whatever happened to the anticipation of a relaxing soak in the tub, surrounded by soothing music, soft candle-light, and a glass of champagne? Maybe I'm just dreaming.

In 2007, we replaced the entire fourteen- by thirty-two-foot deck and log railings due to rotting. After many seasons, twigs and leaf debris had accumulated between the boards and started to decay. The log railings that had been constructed from local tamarack had begun to deteriorate badly no matter how much wood protection I had brushed on them. Tamarack had been a poor choice. We replaced the cedar decking with treated lumber and made sure to leave an adequate gap between boards for drainage. The following year we hired a contractor to install a new ventilated roof after the breakdown of our so-called twenty-five-year shingles. Just recently, we completed the construction of our customized walk-in closet in the master bedroom. Both bedrooms and the loft on the second floor have been carpeted along with the stairway. After waiting nearly twenty years, living out of a few chests of drawers, it felt luxurious finally to enjoy some of the simple domestic pleasures we had anticipated for so long.

From the start in 1990, we had imposed a construction deadline lasting two-and-a-half to three years. The entire project would no doubt be wrapped up by then, and we could move on with our other plans. Then we started moving the goal posts further away. In reality, that timeline stretched out little by little, first to the year 2000; then I promised myself we would complete things by the time Travis finished high school (2005), then by the time the kids graduated from college; finally, by the time we would have our first grandchild; OK, who was I kidding? I would never finish building this damned house in my natural lifetime. Had I become my own version of the mythological Sisyphus, rolling a boulder uphill for eternity only to have it roll down again just before reaching the top? Or did it just seem that way?

It has taken the better part of twenty-five years to get this far, but my consolation is that several of my friends have also been working on their houses for many years. They are still building closets, trimming windows, and running electrical wires. To me, in kind of a perverse way, that actually feels good. It's encouraging to know I have something in common with other long-term do-it-yourselfers. If nothing else, I've learned that if you want quality work, there is no point in rushing the job just to finish it. Patience and persistence are virtues, if not necessities. Although the entire building process seemed to stretch out for an eternity, I always believed it would eventually all come together.

For a very long time, my wife and I have followed a creative and often impractical bent. In some ways, we are a pair of romantic dreamers, chasing after idealized business schemes and artistic goals that seem to make practical sense only on paper. We trust our gut instincts implicitly. Perhaps we are simply following the advice of Thoreau, who in a letter to Harrison Blake once wrote, "Do what you love. Know your own bone; gnaw at it, bury it, unearth it, and gnaw it still."[42] So many years down the road now, we are still gnawing. Music, for example, has always been a big part of our lives: Judy plays guitar, and I play drums and percussion. For many years, we have played in a variety of bands, from rock and country to folk and eclectic, and enjoy jamming regularly with our musical friends. We will never get rich off of it, but then, most musicians play mainly for the love of it.

When the two of us graduated from college, our employment prospects were not exactly glowing. She was a theater major and I an art-and-design major—two of the most unlikely and impractical ways imaginable of approaching the job market. We led with our heart and soul and hoped the details would someday work themselves out. In fact, we have given our sons similar advice: Follow your passion, and even if you don't make a fortune, you will love your work. I hope we haven't steered them into an artistic life of poverty. Well into their twenties now, both of my sons have their share of school debt and concerns about their job prospects to grapple with, but they are on the right path. Maybe they both have a less romantic, more down-to-earth view of life. Time will tell.

For many years, on the north side of our property, facing

Lake Superior and the Canadian shoreline, stood a giant poplar tree, some seventy-five-feet tall and about eighteen inches in diameter. Before starting construction on the house years earlier, we had chain-sawed most trees that might interfere with the building site, saving as many maples and birches as possible. Once the house was up, taking down a threatening tree without dropping it accidentally on the house became a daunting challenge. This giant poplar loomed in our backyard for years, leaning ever so slightly toward the house, which was only fifteen feet away, because we felt too nervous to cut it down. When the strong winds of October blew in off the lake from the northwest, we would lay upstairs at night in our beds listening to the gale just outside our window, the branches trembling and the tall poplar tree trunk groaning. At any moment, we thought, that poplar might snap like a twig, crash through our roof, and pin us to the bed. We'll have to reach for a cellphone and call in the Jaws of Life to extract us from our predicament, assuming we are still alive.

Of all the trees in the forest, poplar trees are perhaps the most brittle; they have been known to break off midway up the trunk in a powerful wind. The roots are fairly shallow compared to other species and cannot be trusted as an anchor in a strong gust. Many times over the years, my brother Fred and I studied the best way to take this tree down without incurring serious damage. We thought of putting up a forty-foot extension ladder to tie off a strong rope high in the tree, allowing us to muscle it away from the house during the final cut. But again, our experience taught us that some trees don't always fall in the direction one expects. Most are predictable, but not all. If we were wrong, we stood to lose a great deal. *Is it worth the gamble?* we wondered. Without a doubt, our insurance company would have laughed us out of the office for a claim of accidentally dropping a tree on our own house. Even some of our neighbors weighed in with various methods of winching the poplar off to one side with cables before making the big cut. But in the end, we put it off, year after year, an obvious case of neglectful procrastination.

Finally, I called several professional tree-trimmers in town for an estimate. I told them that all they had to do was drop the tree safely in the yard, no sawing into pieces, no cleanup; I would take it from there. One guy gave me an estimate of $1,200; he claimed the steep price was due to the insurance he carried, just in case the tree hit the house. His pricey offer only aggravated my anxiety, so I let it pass.

A couple of years later, just before the blustery winds of October blew in again, I called another ad I had seen in the newspaper. This fellow came out the next day and bid $150 to drop my nightmare to the ground. Excitedly, I asked how soon he could start. He attached his climbing spikes to his boots and wrapped a strap around the tree to his waist, then shinnied up to the treetop. Using a very small chainsaw, he carefully sawed off one limb after another and let them fall. With the help of a rope, his helper sent him up a larger saw, which he used to cut down the remaining trunk one piece at a time. When nothing but a twenty-foot post was left, the nimble tree-trimmer climbed back down and sawed the last threatening piece. In a matter of thirty minutes flat, he had slain the menacing beast that had intimidated us for fifteen years. We gained a great deal of respect for the savvy of an experienced woodsman and slept much more soundly every night. Let the wind howl now; we didn't care.

My wife and I have discovered that it pays to be frugal, not just in regard to building the house, but in many other aspects of our lives. Both of us came from families that had little to spare and, as we grew older, learned to respect the value of hard-earned money. The wiser our spending habits, the longer the money would last. From the first day we married, we became avid garage sale fanatics, tracking down bargain furniture that we could easily repair and refinish. We shopped for used clothing at Goodwill and the Salvation Army and read sale flyers to find the best buys every week on food. Like most couples starting out, we went through our share of cheap clunker automobiles, driving only what we could afford at the time. Not wanting to waste our money paying interest to a bank for an auto loan, we tried to save our money until we had enough to buy a decent set of wheels. To this day, we see no need ever to purchase a brand new car when a vehicle three-to-five years old usually has a long life ahead of it. Cars are made to be so much more reliable today that running them to 200,000 miles is not out of the question. We think of it all as a form of recycling—clothes, furniture, cars—the more we do, the better it is for our limited natural resources. For now, we have no desire to live totally off the grid. But it's still reassuring to know that everything old can be new again.

Trying to keep up with the Joneses is pointless. Greater, more rewarding dreams can be chased. As Sarah Susanka suggests in her book, *The Not So Big House*:

> When we have what the Joneses have, we experience firsthand the inadequacy of the dream. There is a deep yearning for something more. The paradox is that that something more resides in less. More quality, less quantity. More beauty, less bravado. More inner abundance, less outer display of wealth.[43]

Every individual has a choice to make as far as what to spend his or her money on. Unfortunately, consumer spending is what drives the economy of this country, so many jobs depend upon it. And yet, the lessons of growing up in the U.P. have not been completely lost on us. Learning to be more resourceful and self-sufficient has its rewards: you save money and develop valuable lifelong skills.

From time to time, I run across people who ask me about my experience building this log home. Sometimes, they are just curious, or else they are considering building one themselves, possibly as a retirement home. The advice I give is usually something like what Ben Franklin once said when it came to love and marriage: "Keep your eyes wide open before marriage, half-shut afterwards." In other words, perform your due diligence; inform yourself by learning as much as you can about the pros and cons of log home construction and the many variables involved. Know what you are getting into as much as possible by asking many questions and talking to a variety of sources. But once the house is built, learn to accept a few imperfections, things that don't turn out exactly as expected. If you enjoy a good night's sleep, keep in mind that there are much worse things to worry about.

In some ways, our experience was a trial by fire in which we finally came to realize our physical and emotional limits. It taught us about resilience and humility. We rediscovered the value of a good sense of humor in riding out everyday rough spots, especially during times when Murphy's Law seemed to take over. I have come to the conclusion that human beings are stubborn creatures—damned stubborn—and reluctant to admit a mistake. We take a stab at something without totally foreseeing where that decision might lead. It happens every day in our relationships with one another; it happens in politics; it happens in business. We try to make it up as we go along. By the time we realize we've made the wrong choice, we've gone too far. It's too late to turn back, so we just muddle through and try to straighten things out as best we can.

Humans are comical in some ways, but determined to get their way, come what may. Instead of admitting to a mistake early on, we compound the error by doubling down. It's as if some invisible force drives us relentlessly onward, with the promise that we can pick up the pieces later. That behavior may be a bit reckless and cavalier, but, as humans, we are no doubt still evolving and will never be perfect. Comical? Sure. Stubborn? No question. Highly intelligent? Not so much.

Journal Entries:

"In Sault Ste. Marie one is entirely locked in for five or six months in a prison of ice and snow." [44]

— Bishop Baraga, the Snowshoe Priest, January 1862

3/16/2010—Set a new spring record for "earliest date to drive up to the house." March 13, we drove both cars the full length of the driveway and parked near our front door. All winter long, we shovel a hundred-foot path from the street to the house. Winter, for the first time in memory, hardly showed up for the main event this year. We are about forty-five inches below our seasonal snowfall average; I haven't even picked up a snow shovel since late January and didn't have to shovel my roof off this winter—unheard of in the U.P. Spring is a good month ahead of schedule this year; it kind of makes up for the twenty-below-zero winters with endless snowfall that we've had in the past. I'm trying not to feel guilty. Then why do I feel that somehow we're going to wind up paying for this?

4/17/2011—First day of driving all the way up to the house this spring: April 9th. All the snow was just about melted; then I awoke this morning to three inches of cold white slop on the ground, accompanied by howling winds. Since I had already retired my snow shovels for the winter, I cleared the porch steps with a leaf rake instead, and it worked quite well. The good news is that I didn't have to shovel my roof this past winter, for the second year in a row. Are we being spoiled?

4/12/2013—This is our twentieth winter living in our log home out here on Walton Bay. I have hand-shoveled the walk, the driveway, and the roof every one of those years. (The three previous winters were rather mild and didn't require roof shoveling.) But this is the first year I have ever felt the need to count my days of shoveling snow. As of April 12 of this year, I have shoveled twenty-nine times! I'm hoping that the six inches of snow we had last night will be the last of the season. This winter has gone on for far too long. The first robin I saw on Easter (March 31) has retreated temporarily to await better nest-building conditions.

11/20/2014—Last week, on November 10, we parked our cars at the end of the driveway in anticipation of our first winter storm. It did not disappoint. Within the next three days, we had accumulated over twenty-nine inches of snow. After a three-day respite, we are back at it again this week: shovel, shovel, shovel. We're expecting up to ten inches today with 30 mph winds. All the schools are closed, for the second time in ten days, and it's not even Thanksgiving yet. So we closed the business for the day. Good day for reading, putting up the Christmas tree, and, of course . . . shoveling.

Here on the southern shore of Izaak Walton Bay in the Upper St. Mary's River, our log home looks across the water to Canada. This is our Walden Pond. Out on the bay, thousand-foot ore freighters from Duluth and Marquette work their way downbound to the steel mills in Chicago and ports on Lake Erie. In summer weather, sailboats and small fishing vessels ply these waters for recreation.

My wife and I take our kayaks out for a paddle to Cedar Point near a nest of bald eagles. Such free-spirited, magnificent birds, their wingspans reaching nearly eight feet, they soar over our bay each summer in search of fish. On a warm day, we stop sometimes for a swim in one of the sandy coves along the way. Occasionally, we make it over toward Sand Island, to our northeast, where the river current picks up speed, due to the narrowing of the channel, and the waves grow choppier. Sand Island is a fertile oasis in the middle of the shimmering river, beckoning boaters and picnickers. They like to drop anchor here for a cool swim and a close-up view of the passing freighters.

Our beach is sandy, but quite narrow—about eight to twelve feet deep, depending on the seasonal level of Lake Superior. Dried-up, twisted logs and driftwood wash up on the shore, especially in the fall when the wave action gets a bit livelier. Over the years, we've lost one rubber raft, an aluminum canoe, and two fourteen-foot rowboats on this shallow shoreline. I have made the mistake of not removing them from the beach to higher ground by the time the vigorous fall weather sets in, usually about the first week of October. The waves at that time of year pound the shoreline with a vengeance, sometimes all night long. Any watercraft situated on the beach gets slammed around relentlessly. The neglected raft was a shredded mess the morning we found it, the canoe so mangled I gave it away to someone who planned to rebuild it. One boat was so savagely mutilated that we sawed it in half and dragged it up the hundred-foot hill to take to a landfill. After a few years, we finally realized that the only type of watercraft that made any sense in this particular location was a kayak. It is light enough to carry a few feet up the hillside for safe storage. Plus, a kayak is just plain fun to cruise across the bay in and, being motorless, very friendly to the environment.

On the hillside, a few feet above the beach, we built a small eight-by-ten-foot platform. It sits just beneath a trio of sheltering cedars we refer to as the Three Sisters. Late on a fall afternoon, when the mosquitoes and black flies have retreated for the season, we relax there with a glass of wine and watch the Canada geese and wood ducks feeding in the shallow bay. A field of golden reeds waves in the breeze and offers cover to a school of hungry minnows. It's a great place to measure the passage of time.

As winter settles in by mid-January, the bay is transformed into a colony of ice-fishing shacks. Some are set in three feet of water; others are placed out near the shipping channel at twenty-foot depths. Most of the fishermen head out to their shanties by snowmobile at first light. On a good day, they catch several whitefish and an occasional northern pike.

By late March, most of the shanties disappear as the spring thaw approaches. The first Great Lakes ore freighter is allowed to pass through the Soo Locks on March twenty-fifth each year, the official beginning of the shipping season. Spotting the first few freighters of spring is always a hopeful sign, for locals, of warmer weather to come—and the perennial anticipation of backyard barbecues, boating, and abundant gardens.

None of the amenities that we enjoy came to us overnight. But now, after such a long struggle, we savor them every day and are grateful. Relaxing in an Adirondack chair on the back porch, facing the Upper St. Mary's River, I can't help but think what a sweet place this is to watch the world go by.

Sometimes, we start out daydreaming and wondering—*What if?* Our imagination takes over and soon, we are lost in reverie. If we are lucky, the long journey begins and leads us on an adventure that will not only breathe new life into us, but change us forever.

Notes

1. Kidder, Tracy. *House*. New York: Houghton Mifflin Company, 1985; Mariner Books, 1999. p. 279.
2. Pollan, Michael. *A Place of My Own: The Education of an Amateur Builder*. New York: Random House, 1997. p. 7.
3. Bachelard, Gaston. *The Poetics of Space*. Boston: Beacon Press, 1969.
4. Susanka, Sarah. *The Not So Big House: A Blueprint for the Way We Really Live*. Newtown, CT: The Taunton Press, 1998. p. 134, 136.
5. Skjelver, Mabel Cooper. *Nineteenth Century Homes of Marshall, Michigan*. Marshall, MI: Marshall Historical Society, 1971. p. xi.
6. Gallagher, John. *Great Architecture of Michigan*. Detroit: Michigan Architectural Foundation, 2008. p. 152.
7. Pollan, *A Place of My Own*, p. 136.
8. Kidder, *House*, p. 133-134.
9. Pollan, *A Place of My Own*, p. 148.

10. Kidder, *House*, p. 134-135.

11. Huttenstine, Jan McAdams. *Remotely Yours: A Historic Journey into the Whitefish Point Area*. Paradise, MI: East West Press LLC, 2010. p. 31.

12. Bohnak, Karl. *So Cold A Sky: Upper Michigan Weather Stories*. Negaunee, MI: Cold Sky Publishing, 2006. p. 55.

13. Arbic, Bernie & Steinhaus, Nancy. *Upbound Downbound: The Story of the Soo Locks*. Allegan Forest, MI: Priscilla Press, 2005. p. 15.

14. Ibid., p. 21-22.

15. Bohnak, *So Cold A Sky*, p. 56.

16. Ibid., p. 56.

17. Hill, Richard. *Lake Effect: A Deckhand's Journey on the Great Lakes Freighters*. Sault Ste. Marie, MI: Gale Force Press, 2008. p. 43.

18. Larson, Amanda Wiljanen. *Finnish Heritage in America*. (Marquette, MI: Delta Kappa Gamma Society, 1976. p. 21.

19. Ibid., p. 22.

20. Crowe, William S. *Lumberjack: Inside An Era in the Upper Peninsula of Michigan*. 3d ed. Edited by Lynn McGlothlin Emerick & Ann McGlothlin Weller. Skandia, MI: North Country Publishing, 2002. p. 13.

21. Ibid., p. 13.

22. Ibid., p. 17.

23. Ibid., p. 74.

24. Ibid., p. 94.

25. Hoadley, R. Bruce. *Understanding Wood: A Craftsman's Guide to Wood Technology*. Newtown, CT: The Taunton Press, 1980. p. 229.

26. Ibid., p. 229.

27. Ibid., p. 229.

28. Ibid., p. 229.

29. Sloane, Eric. *A Reverence for Wood*. New York: Funk & Wagnalls, 1965. p. 29.

30. Ibid., p. 72.

31. Pollan, *A Place of My Own*, p. 172.

32. Thoreau, Henry David. *Walden, or Life in the Woods*. Boston: Ticknor and Fields, 1854. Reprint. Boston: Beacon Press, 1997. p. 303.

33. Susanka, *The Not So Big House*, p. 10.

34. Faulkner, William. *Requiem for a Nun*. New York: Random House, 1951.

35. Thoreau, *Walden*, p. 305.

36. Ibid., p. 76.

37. Pollan, *A Place of My Own*, p. 124.

38. Ibid., p. 124.

39. Bohnak, *So Cold A Sky*, p. 195.

40. Gawande, Atul. *Being Mortal: Medicine and What Matters in the End.* New York: Henry Holt and Company, Metropolitan Books, 2014. p. 97.

41. Stengel, Richard. "Mandela: His 8 Lessons of Leadership." *Time.* 9 July 2008.

42. Richardson Jr., Robert D. *Henry Thoreau: A Life of the Mind.* 1986. Berkeley and Los Angeles, CA: University of California Press; London, England: University of California Press, Ltd., 1998, p. 188.

43. Susanka, *The Not So Big House*, p. 184.

44. Bohnak, *So Cold A Sky*, p. 110.

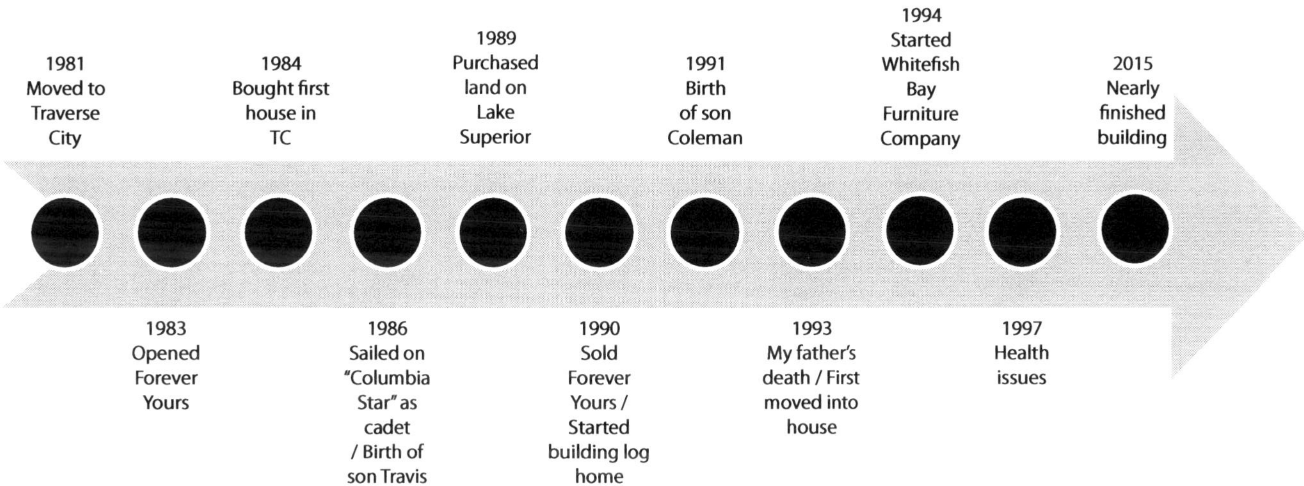
1981 Moved to Traverse City
1983 Opened Forever Yours
1984 Bought first house in TC
1986 Sailed on "Columbia Star" as cadet / Birth of son Travis
1989 Purchased land on Lake Superior
1990 Sold Forever Yours / Started building log home
1991 Birth of son Coleman
1993 My father's death / First moved into house
1994 Started Whitefish Bay Furniture Company
1997 Health issues
2015 Nearly finished building

Timeline

Acknowledgments

In writing this book, I would like to thank a few people for their help and encouragement. First I want to thank my wife Judy, not only for reading and commenting on some of the early chapters, but also for reminding me of many story details I might have forgotten. It's been a long, eventful, and pleasurable journey together. For reading some of the early drafts and offering some very helpful structuring ideas, I want to thank my brother Jim Hill. His wise suggestions and questions helped smooth over many bumps along the road. Many thanks to Tyler Tichelaar for his fine editing skills; I didn't realize I could split that many infinitives. My appreciation to Stacey Willey at Globe Printing for her deft layout and design skills as well as her professional manner. And, of course, my gratitude to the carpenters, plumbers, electricians and others who helped make this log house a reality. Lastly, my great thanks to my brother Fred Hill for his selfless efforts in the most difficult parts of this project. And cheers to all my family members for their never-ending encouragement and their love for telling great stories—no matter how late the hour.

Log Building Resources

Since we started the construction of our log home in 1990, quite a number of things have changed. The accessibility of the Internet, more than anything, has opened up a broad spectrum of resources and information on log home building. Now at our fingertips is an endless source for log-building tools, plans, techniques, kits, supplies, log furniture, décor, furnishings, as well as YouTube videos.

For a long list of books about log homes, your local bookstore or library is a good place to start. Otherwise, there is a wide choice of material on Amazon.com or BarnesandNoble.com. On the newsstand are a number of magazines that run monthly photo spreads of lavishly built and decorated log homes, apparently targeted at a wealthy clientele who can afford to drop some serious money on a dream home. Most of these magazines—*Log Home Living, Cabin Living*, or *Timber Home Living*—also feature many resources for log home manufacturers, décor, and supplies. They serve as a useful tool to explore many design possibilities and details.

Once your dream home is completed, the next thing to keep in mind is regular maintenance: sealing cracks, preventing water and insect penetration, cleaning the log surface occasionally, and renewing the finish every few years. Sometimes, there are tears in the chinking to be repaired and checks or cracks in the logs that must be filled. Numerous companies online sell maintenance supplies such as: LogFinish.com and

TimelessWoodCare.com. They carry everything from latex chinking and log finishes to foam backer rod and epoxy kits for repairing rotted logs.

Most importantly, if you plan to build any kind of log home, educate yourself. And don't believe everything a manufacturer tells you; skepticism is often healthy. Talk to other people who have had direct experience either building themselves or those who have lived in a log home for some length of time. Do-it-yourselfers will usually give you an honest appraisal of their experience, pros and cons. It would also be helpful to check several online forums of people who have built with logs or dealt with various log home manufacturers. Take the time to visit different log homes in your area and talk to their owners. Ask lots of probing questions. Schools around the country offer classes on log building that last anywhere from two to ten days. Hands-on experience can be a great supplement to simply reading books about building. So much valuable time and expense is involved in designing and completing a log home that it doesn't pay to rush the process. Before committing to any firm decision, take your time and inform yourself thoroughly on all the issues involved. In the end, building your log home will be a peak learning and life experience. For the sake of greater satisfaction and peace of mind, a dream should start off on the right foot.

Building Terms Glossary

AIR-DRIED LUMBER – Wood dried without artificial heat, only by exposure to air, generally by stacking in yards or sheds. Alternative is kiln-dried lumber.

BACKER ROD – Foam filler or backing used in caulking or chinking to reduce the amount of sealant necessary; also serves as an expansion joint so the caulk is not pulled away from the log.

BEARING WALL – A wall that supports an upper floor or wall.

BOARD FOOT – Lumber measurement equivalent to 144 cubic inches, or the amount of lumber contained in a piece 1" thick, 12" wide, and 12" long or its equivalent.

BTU – British Thermal Unit. One BTU is the quantity of heat required to raise the temperature of one pound of water by one degree Fahrenheit. Used in the heating, ventilation, and air conditioning (HVAC) industry.

BUCK – A vertical board fastened to the ends of log sections at the window or door openings to secure them in place and to which the window or doorjamb is fastened.

BUTT – The large end of a log or the base of a felled tree.

BUTT AND PASS – Term used to describe the corners formed when one log stops or butts and the other log extends past the corner or passes. The corners alternate as they progress upward.

CAULKING – Material used to seal the joints between logs or between windows and walls, doors and walls, etc.

CHECKING – A surface crack in a log caused by drying.

CHINKING – Filler used to cover the larger seams between rows of logs.

DIMENSIONAL LUMBER – Typical lumber such as 2 x 4. It is nominally 2 inches thick (actually 1½") and 4 inches wide (actually 3½").

"D" LOG – An engineered or milled log with a "D" shape, where the outside of the log is rounded and the inside is flat.

DOOR BUCK – Framed rough opening to install a finished door assembly.

DORMER – A window or a smaller roofed area protruding from a sloping roof.

DOUBLE-HUNG WINDOW – Windows with an upper and lower sash, both of which can be opened.

DRAW-KNIFE – A woodworking tool with a knife-edged blade set between two handles. It is used by drawing it along a log to peel the bark or shave it down.

DRY ROT – Term used to indicate rotten, crumbly wood. Actually a misnomer since the fungi that cause the damage require moisture.

DRYWALL – Panels or sheets of paper-covered plaster for wall and ceiling coverings. It's also made without the paper for reduced mold and mildew.

ELEVATION – The point of view of the structure from the ground outside, e.g., front elevation or side elevation.

FASCIA – Finish board applied to the edge of the roof on the eaves and gables.

FLOOR JOISTS – Framing that supports the floor by resting on lower walls, girders, or beams.

FOOTING or FOOTER – Wide concrete slab underneath perimeter of a slab or foundation walls, set on virgin soil.

FOUNDATION – Lower bearing wall that transfers the load of a building to the footers and ground, usually made of poured concrete, concrete block, or pressure-treated wood.

GABLE – Triangular-shaped section of end walls underneath the peak of the roof line.

GENERAL CONTRACTOR – Person responsible for the overall coordination, planning, hiring, and supervision of a building project.

GREEN WOOD – Usually used to refer to a recently-cut tree, it is technically wood that has a fiber moisture content of 28 percent or higher.

HAND-PEELING – The process of removing the bark of a log by hand, generally with a draw-knife. Sometimes, some of the inner or cambium layer is left, called skip-peeling.

HEARTH – Area in front of a fireplace; can be raised or flat.

KILN-DRIED – Forced, artificial drying of logs or lumber to reach a certain moisture content, typically 15 percent or less.

LAG BOLT – A large metal fastener with a hex head and screw threads that drive it into the wood, as opposed to bolt threads, which tighten with a nut; should technically be called a lag screw.

LOG GRADING – The process whereby logs are inspected and graded, indicating defects in the wood and its suitability for certain applications.

LOG PACKAGE – The logs and materials provided by a log home manufacturer to erect the basic structure, a weather-tight home or a complete turnkey package. Can include materials lists and blueprints, but rarely the actual construction service, unless it's handcrafted.

LOG PROFILE – The cross-sectional shape of a log. Can be "D" shape, round, beveled, or flat.

LOG SIDING – Exterior siding made of strips cut from a log; imitates the look of a log structure.

MILLED LOGS – Logs that have been shaped and smoothed by a machine to a uniform size and shape, as opposed to handcrafted logs.

MOISTURE CONTENT – The amount of water remaining in wood, usually expressed as a percentage. The fiber saturation point at which wood shrinkage begins is about 28 percent moisture content.

MORTISE – A square or rectangular slot cut into a log, timber, or board into which another member, usually called a tenon, will fit.

MORTISE AND TENON JOINT – A joint in which a projection (tenon) of one timber is inserted into a slot (mortise) of another timber.

NON-BEARING WALL – Any wall that supports only its own weight.

NOTCH – An angle or divot cut into a log, especially used at corners to interlock them for strength and weather-resistance.

OSB – Stands for "Oriented Strand Board," an engineered alternative to plywood made of wood fibers pressed and glued together.

PERCOLATION (OR "PERC") TEST – A test to determine how quickly water will percolate or be absorbed into the ground.

PITCH – The slope or angle of a roof; also, the hardened sap of a coniferous tree.

PLUMB – In a vertical line, straight up and down.

POST-AND-BEAM CONSTRUCTION – Construction where wall support is provided by vertical posts and horizontal beams.

PRESSURE TREATED – A method of treating wood by forcing a preservative liquid into the wood cells under pressure.

PURLINS – A roof support log reaching from end to end of the structure and placed in line between plate log and the ridgepole. Usually, it is used to support rafters.

RAFTERS – Framing members spanning from ridge to eave that support the roof.

RIDGE BEAM – A structural beam or engineered lumber designed to support the upper ends of the rafters and carry the roof load along with the walls. Also called a ridge board, ridge piece, or ridgepole.

RISER – The vertical span between two horizontal stair treads.

ROOF DECKING – Sheathing of plywood or OSB installed on rafters.

ROOFING FELT – Asphalt building paper installed on roof sheathing underneath shingles.

ROUGH-IN – Installation of basic construction framing, electrical, plumbing, or HVAC components inside the walls before finishing.

ROUGH OPENING – Slightly over-sized opening in building frame for windows, doors, etc., leaving enough room to shim the components plumb, level, and square.

ROUGH-SAWN – Lumber that has been sawn but not planed smooth. Saw marks often show on face and lumber is oversize from standard.

R-VALUE – A measure of a material's resistance to heat flow. The higher the number, the greater the insulating capability.

SADDLE-NOTCH CORNERS – Method of handling log corners where the upper log has a notch cut in the shape of a saddle, which rests over the bottom log. Also known as saddle cope or round notch.

SCRIBE – The process of cutting one log to match the contours of another for a tight log-to-log fit.

SETTLING – Downward movement of logs and log walls as they dry out and as more weight is added.

SHEATHING – Plywood or OSB installed over framing to provide a flat surface for siding or roofing and to act as racking resistance.

SHRINKAGE – The movement of lumber or logs as they dry out.

SINGLE-HUNG WINDOW – A window with only one sash that opens.

SLOPE – The incline of a roof. It is rise (in inches) over run (of 12 inches). For a 24' wide house with a rise of 12', the slope is a 12-in-12. Often erroneously used interchangeably with pitch.

SQUARE – Refers to a 90-degree corner, also a unit of measure for roofing. It is shorthand for the amount of roofing needed to cover 100 sq. ft.

STICK-BUILT – Conventional construction, built of studs or "sticks."

STUD – Wood framing members, providing the support in a wall system.

STRUCTURAL INSULATED PANELS or SIPs – High-performance panels made up of an insulated foam core sandwiched between structural skins of OSB. Can be used for floors, roofs, and walls.

SUB-CONTRACTOR – Tradesman hired by a general contractor to handle specific tasks of a build.

SUB-FLOOR – Rough floor deck of plywood or OSB. Finish floor is installed over this.

SWEDISH COPE (also called Scandinavian Scribe) – Method of cutting concave section on upper log to rest on the convex portion of lower log.

TENON – An extension at the end of a piece of timber or log cut to fit into an accommodating, same-size mortise. A tenon can be round, square, or rectangular.

THERMAL MASS – The insulating property of a solid wall such as logs, whereby heat is absorbed and slowly released over time.

TIMBER FRAMING – Traditional construction method where the braced frame supporting the structure is visible and made of large timbers.

TONGUE & GROOVE (T&G) – Lumber with a projection or tongue on one side and a corresponding groove on the other.

TREADS – Horizontal boards that act as steps in a stairway.

TRUNNEL – Shortened version of "tree nail." A trunnel is a large wooden peg or dowel used to secure two pieces of wood together. Often used in timber-framing to hold joints.

TURNKEY – Ready to move into, all aspects of the build are handled by one entity.

UNDERLAYMENT – Sheet material installed under floor coverings to provide a smooth surface.

WINDOW BUCK – Framed rough opening to install a window unit.

Sources

International Log Builders' Association

www.logassociation.org

Log Cabin Connection

www.log-cabin-connection.com

About the Author

Rich Hill lives along the shore of Lake Superior in Michigan's Eastern Upper Peninsula with his wife Judy and their cocker spaniel Maxwell. He graduated from Northern Michigan University with a BFA in Art and Design. Jamming occasionally with other local musicians, Rich plays conga drums and bongos, mostly for their portability. Out in his garage workshop, Rich spends his time woodworking and bringing older pieces of neglected furniture back to life. He has published two other books thus far: *Lake Effect: A Deckhand's Journey on the Great Lakes Freighters* and *Hitchhiking After Dark: Offbeat Stories from a Small Town* (1st place winner in humor at the Midwest Book Awards). He can be contacted by emailing moosician@exede.net.

For additional copies visit:
www. GaleForcePress.com
Address all inquiries to:
Richard Hill
5480 W Cedar Drive, Sault Ste. Marie, MI 49783
906-632-8104 • email: moosician@exede.net